EASTER RISING:

THE LAST WORDS OF PATRICK PEARSE

EASTER RISING:

THE LAST WORDS OF PATRICK PEARSE

**A DRAMATIC MONOLOGUE
IN THREE ACTS by
BRIAN GORDON SINCLAIR**

THE NEW ATLANTIAN LIBRARY

is an imprint of
Absolutely Amazing eBooks.

Published by Whiz Bang LLC, 926 Truman Avenue, Key West, Florida 33040, USA.

For information, contact:
Publisher@AbsolutelyAmazingEbooks.com

ISBN-13: 978-0692655726 (New Atlantian Library, The)
ISBN-10: 0692655727

Easter Rising: The Last Words of Patrick Pearse
is dedicated to the memory of
Turlough Breathnach*
for he was a guide to all that was Pearse.
Through knowledge, passion and kindness
he was the light of inspiration.

*Turlough Breathnach was curator of the Pearse Museum,
St. Enda's Park, Rathfarnham, Ireland.

PERFORMANCE RIGHTS

For the first time, with this publication, performances will be allowed by groups or individuals other than the author. No performance, other than by Brian Gordon Sinclair, may be given unless a license has been obtained from the author. No alterations may be made to the title or the text without prior written permission from the author.

The original production of *Easter Rising: The Last Words of Patrick Pearse* was multi-media and employed a series of twin slide projections and a soundtrack. Slides and sound effects are not available from the author. All sound effects, however, are present in the audio book version and may, with the permission of the author, be incorporated into a presentation; otherwise, independent producers are responsible for obtaining projections and sound effects. Please note that the play works extremely well as a monologue and can be produced without the addition of slides and sound effects thus making the show extremely portable for travel.

For information, contact:
Publisher@AbsolutelyAmazingEbooks.com

EASTER RISING:

THE LAST WORDS OF PATRICK PEARSE

CONTENTS

INTRODUCTION I
EASTER RISING:
ACT ONE 1
ACT TWO 31
ACT THREE 47
ABOUT THE AUTHOR AND HIS WORKS 77
PHOTO GALLERY 79
OTHER WORKS BY
BRIAN GORDON SINCLAIR:
THE HEMINGWAY MONOLOGUES   96
HEMINGWAY'S HOT HAVANA   99
CUBA SOLIDARIY IN CANADA   100
THE PIRATE NIGHT BEFORE
CHRISTMAS   101
THE HOMERUN KID   102
SPECIAL INVITATION   103
REVIEWS   107

INTRODUCTION

A MEMORY OF HEROISM ... A FUTURE OF PEACE!

BACKGROUND: The death of a parent is a seminal event in each and every life. With the passing of my Irish born mother came the loving recollection of a strong woman who raised me in a cold water flat, cleaned houses for a living, cared for a war wounded husband and coped with the frustrations of an all-male family. Inherent in her was the will to survive and an indomitable fighting spirit, a spirit that is common to the Irish people. At this time, a desire to know more about this spirit and to explore my roots was kindled.

This desire became enflamed by the discovery of an incredible historical event, the Irish revolution of 1916. The events of the Rising combined to form one of the great dramas of our time. Amazingly no one, until now, had ever written a theatrical drama detailing this adventure much less presenting it from the viewpoint of its leader, Patrick H. Pearse – poet, lawyer, visionary, educationalist and rebel.

HISTORICAL SIGNIFICANCE: The 1916 Irish Easter uprising was the first successful revolution in 20th century Europe. A courageous band of revolutionaries, though scorned by most of their fellow Irishmen were convinced that through their defeat and deaths they would arouse the Irish people to a victorious fight for independence. Incredibly, they were right and out of the Easter Rising came a resurgence of the Irish nationalism which led ultimately to Irish independence, the Irish Free State in 1922 and the Republic of Ireland in 1948.

RESEARCH: Six weeks in Ireland allowed me to walk in the literal footsteps of the heroes of 1916 and to come into contact with the most helpful group of people I have ever encountered – Pat Cooke and Turlough Breathnach at the Pearse museum, Niamh O'Sullivan at the Kilmainham Jail Museum and Michael Kenny at the National Museum of Ireland. Costume sketches were prepared by artist/historian F. Glen Thompson and a multitude of original documents and books were assembled. This material was digested and revised over a period of 18 months resulting in a final script, ready for rehearsal, in the early months of 2000.

REHEARSAL PROCESS: As each scene was methodically workshopped with moment-to-moment precision, Mary Logan and her team of Stratford Festival costumers created a precise replica of the Thompson drawing using materials and weaponry purchased in Canada, England and Ireland. At the same time, Stratford sound engineer, Paul Benedict, created a superb soundtrack that included poetry by both P. H. Pearse and W. B. Yeats as well as a wide selection of authentic Irish rebel music.

Simultaneously, over 150 period photos and documents, many provided by Radio Television Erin, were turned into slides. Projectors dissolve units, special lens for rear projection, portable Mylar screens, and a full CD based sound system were assembled. One week prior to the April 24 anniversary of the Rising, all elements were in place. All that remained was a series of successful dress rehearsals prior to the moment when *Easter Rising* would meet its first audience.

THE PERFORMANCE: *Easter Rising* was a solo performer event presented by a Guthrie Award winning actor at the peak of his powers. As the play reached into the hearts and souls of its audience, people actually relived this exciting moment of Irish History. When the performance was over, audience members felt and understood the true purpose of the play - to appreciate the heroism but to be horrified at the bloodshed of war and to join in the author's intention of moving towards a future of peace.

THE RESPONSE: Audience reaction was overwhelmingly enthusiastic. Comments on the multi-media production included the following statements:

"Sinclair becomes the character."

"He exudes passion."

"Sinclair's dramatic delivery has incredible impact."

"Like no other play presented on stage in this area."

"The audience is transported to the heart of Dublin and the uprising."

"Sinclair's final soliloquy moved the audience to tears."

"Sinclair manages to present this incredible and tragic story without depressing the audience. There is something uplifting about the hope and sacrifice of Pearse."

"This story should be read, heard and seen in every country of the world."

EASTER RISING: THE LAST WORDS OF PATRICK PEARSE was originally produced by the "Children of Erin" Theatre Company at the Millpond Centre for the Arts in Alliston, Ontario, Canada on Easter Monday, April 24, 2000.

OF SPECIAL NOTE: In the year 2000, Easter Monday fell on April 24 for the first time since the original Rising in 1916.

Original slide and sound cues are included in this version of *Easter Rising*. SR and SL refer to stage right and stage left.

EASTER RISING:
THE LAST WORDS OF PATRICK PEARSE

ACT ONE

SETTING: The stage is bare except for a chair and table
            stage right and a chest and hat rack stage
            left. Behind the stage are two large
            projection screens. A full length Celtic Cross
            hanging is suspended on each side of the
            screens. Slides and recordings allow the
            actor to be in and around the General Post
            Office, Dublin, Ireland, 1916.

AT RISE: Prior to the act, Rebel music plays for thirty
            minutes. It stops shortly before show time.
            After an appropriate pause, instrumental
            Scarce O'Tatties begins to play. Once the
            music is established, Pearse enters stage
            left. He looks around and moves to the table
            where he prepares. He puts a bullet in the
            revolver and checks his sword and hat.
            When ready, he picks up a copy of the
            proclamation and walks to centre stage
            where he freezes for the last ten seconds of

the music.

(Slide SR - *Easter Rising:*, slide SL - *The Last Words Of Patrick Pearse*. These slides are on prior to the show.)

(Fade to black)

VOICE-OVER

I have met them at close of day
Coming with vivid faces
From counter or desk among grey
Eighteenth-century houses.
I have passed with a nod of the head
Or polite meaningless words,
Or have lingered awhile and said
Polite meaningless words,
And thought before I had done
Of a mocking tale or a gibe
To please a companion
Around the fire at the club,
Being certain that they and I
But lived where motley is worn:
All changed, changed utterly:
A terrible beauty is born.

(A judicial gavel strikes three times and a British military
        judge speaks.)

VOICE-OVER (the judge)

Patrick Henry Pearse, it is clear that you are a traitor to England; therefore, it is the judgment of this court that you will be taken to a place of execution at Kilmainham Gaol where you will face death by firing squad. May God have mercy on your soul.

Mr. Pearse, before being removed to the place of execution, do you have any last words?

(Pearse replies in a soulful echo.)

VOICE-OVER (Pearse)

Yes!

(Soundtrack: drum roll, slide SR. -
POBLACHT NA H EIREANN.
Second drum roll, slide SL - THE
PROVISIONAL GOVERNMENT
OF THE IRISH REPUBLIC TO THE
PEOPLE OF IRELAND. The lights come to
full at the first drum roll.)

PEARSE

IRISHMEN AND IRISHWOMEN: In the name of God and of the dead generations from which she receives her old tradition of nationhood, Ireland, through us, summons her children to her flag and strikes for her freedom.

We declare the right of the people of Ireland to the ownership of Ireland, and to the unfettered control of Irish destinies, to be sovereign and indefeasible. The long usurpation of that right by a foreign people and government has not extinguished the right, nor can it ever be extinguished except by the destruction of the Irish people. In every generation the Irish People have asserted their right to national freedom and sovereignty: six times during the past three hundred years they have asserted it in arms. Standing on that fundamental right and again asserting it in arms in the face of the world, we hereby proclaim the Irish Republic as a Sovereign Independent State, and we pledge our lives and the lives of our comrades-in-arms to the cause of its freedom, of its welfare, and of its exaltation among the nations.

In this supreme hour, the Irish nation must, by its valour and discipline and by the readiness of its children to sacrifice themselves for the common good, prove itself worthy of the august destiny to which it is called.

Signed on Behalf of the Provisional Government,

> (Slide SR - Clarke, MacDiarmada, Pearse, Connolly. Slide SL - MacDonagh, Ceannt, Plunkett)

Thomas J. Clarke, Sean Mac Diarmada, P. H. Pearse, James Connolly, Thomas MacDonagh, Eamonn Ceannt, Joseph Plunkett.

That was my last chance to practice any part of the speech, for today is the day, and the time is now. It is Easter Monday, April 24th, 1916, just before noon, Dublin time.

> (Slide SR - Dublin street scene. Pearse steps forward.)

The sun is shining, the birds are singing, people are out strolling, gossiping, and enjoying the holiday weather, All in all, it is a fine day for a revolution.

> (Pearse takes his sword from the table and sheaths it.)
> (Slide SL - Liberty Hall and Citizen Army, Slide SR - Volunteer Army)

VOICE-OVER (crowd sounds)
Move along now. Get out of the way, you. Put those guns over there. Give me a hand, will you.
Ow, that was my foot. Watch out you bloody eejit.

PEARSE
The troops are mustering at Liberty Hall, headquarters for the local unions where, for the first time, two groups are now united: the Irish Citizen Army, formed from the union ranks, and the Irish Volunteers, formed in response to the northern Protestants. They have become, in one momentous morning, the first Army of the Irish Republic. Commanding the Dublin Brigades is Commandant General James Conolly, labour leader, Marxist, and Irish nationalist.

> (Pearse moves to the table and puts his hat on.)

Full command of all troops throughout the entirety of Ireland has fallen on my shoulders. My name is Patrick H. Pearse, President of the Provisional Government of the Republic of Ireland and Commandant General, Commanding-in-Chief the Army of the Republic.

> (Pearse moves forward. Slide SL - Willie Pearse)

Sounds impressive, doesn't it? But you should have seen us before. We had all arrived by whatever means available: horse, foot, cart, anything that moved. My brother Willie and I rode into town on our bicycles. Not too distinguished for a general, but very inconspicuous.

One group consisted of fifty-six young Irishmen who had come from England. They wanted to fight for Ireland rather than be conscripted and sent to France to die for the British. This morning, their commanding officer roused them out of a good sleep in the suburb of Kimmage and started them on their long march into Dublin. Soon it became obvious that they wouldn't make it on time, but as luck would have it, a tram happened by.

(Slide SR - tram.   Soundtrack: tram bell)

The C. O. halted it and the entire troop herded on board. "Fifty-seven tuppenny fares," he said, "and don't stop until we reach O'Connell Bridge. Needless to say, the other passengers were not amused. One rather commodious, middle-aged lady was particularly upset when she was jolted in the nether regions by the rifle butt of a young volunteer.

"Conductor," she said, "I demand you put these men off the tram"!

He replied, "Would you mind doing that for me, ma'am. I'm a bit busy myself".

"Well, I never!" she fumed.

But she said no more and since the gun of one of the men happened to be pointed at the driver, the tram sped away quite rapidly . . . I do hope you appreciate the fact that they paid for their fares.

(Pearse moves centre)

Although they arrived on time, several of the volunteers

did not come at all. But it wasn't their fault. In our unique Irish way, we had first scheduled the Rising for Easter Sunday, for symbolic reasons. Well that order was countermanded by Eoin MacNeill.

(Pearse points to Slide SL - Eoin MacNeill)

MacNeill is president of the volunteers and he opposes a rising at this time. So naturally I countermanded his countermand and here we are on Easter Monday. This is a very Irish thing.

(Pearse steps forward.)

Now we were ready, at least as ready as we could ever be under the circumstances. And so the brigades moved out as Connolly gave the orders.

VOICE-OVER (Connolly)
First Detachment Citizen's Army, left turn, quick march.
First Detachment Irish Volunteers, left turn, quick march.
Second Detachment Citizen's Army, left turn, quick march.
Second Detachment Irish Volunteers, left turn, quick march.

PEARSE (speaking through the voice-over)
They are on their way to capture key positions throughout the city.
(Slide SR - the west city map, Slide SL - the east city map. Pearse indicates the various locations.)

To the west we will occupy the South Dublin Union, a Workhouse, the Mendicity Institution, a hospice for the poor, and the so-called centre of justice, the Four Courts.

To the north, Gilbey's distillery...Yes, Irish troops in a distillery... and I might point out that I instructed the men to make this a sobering experience.

To the south, we will seize St. Stephen's Green along with the Shelbourne hotel, and Jacob's Biscuit Factory. Further east, Boland's Bakery. At least there will be bread and biscuits to eat.

(Pearse moves right of centre)

Finally, the rest of us formed ranks on the road outside. At the front, myself, to my left, James Connolly and to his left, Commandant General Joseph Mary Plunkett.

(Slide SR - Connolly and Plunkett)

Plunkett is a poet and a fine military strategist. Wrapped around his throat is a surgical bandage from a recent operation. He is, in fact, dying of tuberculosis. Behind us are less than one hundred and fifty men.

(Slide SL - Clarke and MacDermott)

But they include Tom Clarke and Sean MacDermott or MacDiarmada as he wrote it on the proclamation. Both these men are leaders of the Irish Republican Brotherhood. Clarke had spent fifteen years staring at the dark, grey walls of a British prison cell and has vowed never to go to jail again. MacDermott is crippled by polio and needs a cane to walk but his mind is as sharp as they come.

Now our turn had come. Connolly's lips moved to form the order. But at that precise moment, my sister, Mary Brigid, burst from the crowd and seized my arm.

"Come home, Patrick," she said. "Forget all this foolishness".

I took her aside, held her arms and for a long moment looked straight into her eyes.

"Go home, Mary Brigid, go home", I said. "This is war. Go home to our mother."

Tears welled up in her eyes . . . and then she turned and ran sobbing down the street. Now that was embarrassing.

Connolly, thank God, sensed this and quickly gave the order to march.

VOICE-OVER (Connolly)
Battalion, by the left, quick march!

PEARSE (marching in place)
We were on our way to the final destination, to the place where we would establish our headquarters...

(Slide SR - GPO columns and figures)

... the General Post Office, or GPO as it was called in short. Our ragtag company could have passed for the members of a Gilbert and Sullivan operetta performing in *The Pirates of Penzance* ... and we planned to put on quite a show.

Following us are two trucks, one closed cab, two motorcycles, and a green Ford touring car, totally overloaded with supplies: food, rifles, hammers, and grenades. Oh yes, and first aid kits. I imagine we'll need them.

>(Soundtrack: the Angelus bell. Slide SL - the
>Virgin Mary.)

Halt!

That is the Angelus bell ringing for all Dublin. We are being summoned to mid-day prayer and no good Catholic can refuse.

>(Pearse takes out a Rosary and prays.)

The Angel of the Lord declared unto Mary.

>(The other soldiers are heard in the
>background. All dialogue overlaps.)

>VOICE-OVER (overlapping, bells continue)

And she conceived of the Holy Spirit...

Hail Mary, full of grace, the lord is with thee; blessed art thou among women and blessed is the fruit of thy womb, Jesus. Holy Mary, Mother of God, pray for us sinners, now and at the hour of our death...

Behold the handmaid of the Lord...

And the Word was made flesh...

Pray for us, O holy Mother of God...

Let us pray...

>PEARSE (Live. He overlaps the voice-over.)

Pour Forth, we beseech You, O Lord, Your grace into our

Hearts, that we to whom the Incarnation of Christ, Your Son, Was made known by the message of an Angel, may by His Passion and Cross be brought to the glory of His Resurrection, through the same Christ our lord, Amen.

(Voice-over ends. He kisses the cross, puts it in his pocket and marches in place.)

PEARSE
There, now we can get back to the revolution.

(Slide SL - the G P O, full view.)

As we continued marching, people watched without any idea of what was happening. Some children, ragged and dirty from the slums, tagged along behind.

"Where yez marchin' to this time?" they shouted.

Others cheered, some mocked, and some just called us names.

VOICE-OVER (English officer)
Will these bloody fools never tire of marching up and down the streets?

PEARSE
We ignored them.

And then the column arrived in front of the G P O.
Halt!

For a brief moment I felt dwarfed by the eight ionic columns and the three figures on top: Hibernia, Mercury, and Fidelity; just another of Dublin's minor mysteries.

Then Connolly took a deep breath and with a passion that we all felt, he shouted the command:

> VOICE-OVER (Connolly)
> Left turn. The G P O, charge!

> PEARSE
> And we did.

> VOICE-OVER
> Charge! For Ireland! Hurrah! Let's go lads! Ireland! Out of the way. Move over you. Etc.

> PEARSE
The Post Office had remained open for the holiday and business was brisk, until now when a few nervous rifles exploded into the ceiling. Pieces of plaster fell everywhere, but the customers just stood there, paralyzed until Connolly shouted, "Everybody out!" Then they all stampeded for the doors, except for one man who absolutely insisted on buying a stamp. A young volunteer, pale and nervous, with a revolver in his hand, confronted him. "Hands up or I'll blow your heart out". It was at this exact moment that the man decided to leave.

Now we had to secure the building. Orders were issued: "Smash those windows. Barricade the doors!" The men rushed at the big windows with axes, hammers, rifle butts, any heavy object they had. Outside, a shower of glass erupted simultaneously from all sides of the building. Inside, one of the men stopped and stood there, white-faced and trembling. Blood was spurting from a deep gash in his arm. Suddenly, a woman shoved her head through the broken window right in front of him; one of the shawlies from the slums.

VOICE-OVER (Shawlie)
"Aw, did yez cut yerself. Serves ya right for smashin' all the lovely windows".

PEARSE
Go on, get out of here!

Just as we had calmed and bandaged him, a shotgun went off accidentally, barely missing his head, but it did tear into the buttocks of another man a few feet away. Now that was a pain - never mind. We had no doctor yet and we still had to set up an infirmary so we did the best we could with the first aid kits. I didn't think we'd need them this soon. If this keeps up, we won't have anyone left to fight the British.

In the meantime, we continued with the barricades and within a few short minutes, the ground floor looked like the Donnybrook Fair after one of its famous brawls. Everything of size and weight was pushed against the open windows: tables, chairs, mailbags, ledgers, anything that would stop a bullet.

VOICE-OVER (The O'Rahilly)
Pearse!

PEARSE
When I heard my name called, I turned in the direction of the voice. It was The O'Rahilly.

(Slide SR - The O'Rahilly)

As he walked toward me, a silence fell over the GPO. What

was he doing here? This journalist, this chief of his clan had actually supported MacNeill's countermand order. And not only that, he spent all of Easter Sunday delivering the message. That's why our numbers are so small and that's why we left him out of our plans. Now he was here and I was afraid a terrible argument would take place. We're supposed to be fighting the British, not each other. As we stood there scowling at each other, I thought, in spite of everything, "You have to admire a man who tries to stop an uprising and then, when he sees it is inevitable, steps bravely forward to join it." Then, after an interminable silence, The O'Rahilly spoke, "It's madness," he said, "madness; yet it's glorious madness and I want to be a part of it. I helped wind this clock. I've come to hear it ring." The frown disappeared from his face, a hearty cheer filled the room, and we all shook hands as brothers in arms.

Then it was right back to work. We still had to secure the upper floors.

(To an audience member)

"The telegraph room is upstairs," I said to a volunteer named Michael Staines. "Take a party of six men, clear the upper levels and put them in a state of defense.

Slowly and carefully, Staines and his men made their way up the wide staircase until they reached the landing directly opposite the telegraph office. (snap fingers) There was a sound. They turned and found themselves covered by seven rifles in the hands of British soldiers. One of the volunteers, nervous, fired out of instinct, right into the middle of them. Their sergeant took the bullet and collapsed to the floor. No one moved, no one made a sound, and no one fired back They couldn't. They had no ammunition. They were only the Post Office guard. What need could they possibly have for bullets? To my relief, the sergeant had only been grazed in the forehead so I ordered two men to take him, unwillingly, to Jervis Street Hospital.

Now that the upstairs was secure, we established our headquarters on the second floor and cautiously congratulated ourselves. After all, we had survived the first fifteen minutes. Now it was time to let the world know we were here. "James," I said to Connolly, "Let's raise the flags." "Flags?" he said, "Yes, well...and a strange, blank look come over his face and then he called to my aide, a happy little elf of a man named Sean T. O'Kelly. "Are you busy, Sean?" said Connolly. "Not at all, sir," he replied, "after all, there's only a revolution going on."
"Ahem, yes, well I want you to go back to Liberty Hall and pick up a package of flags that we left there."
Can you believe it? We had forgotten to bring the beautiful new ensigns that were to symbolize the birth of our republic. Sean quickly fetched the flags and returned with them in a plain brown paper parcel.

It is almost 12:30, time for the proclamation. Connolly gave two flags to a Volunteer officer with instructions to raise them, in place of the British flags, on the roof.

(Slide SR - Irish Republic flag)

At the Prince's Street corner, we raised a banner that was a green field. On it in Gaelic lettering, gold and white, were the words, "IRISH REPUBLIC". (Move to chest and get the Tricolor.) Countess Markieviecz did the lettering and you might be interested to know that she created that particular shade of gold by adding mustard powder from her kitchen.

> (Slide SL - Tricolor flag. Pearse places a
> real Tricolor on the hat rack pole.)

At the Henry Street corner, we raised the Tricolor: green for the south, orange for Ulster, and a pure white stripe...resting peacefully between the two. (Get hat and proclamation from table.) Only one Tricolor remained, so I put it in the pocket of my greatcoat for safekeeping.

Then Connolly and I stepped out to face the crowd and read the proclamation. They stared at us like the blocks and stones of *Julius Caesar*. I cleared my throat, raised my voice, and read the eloquent words of independence.

> VOICE-OVER (Crowd)

"Takin' over the city are ye? Well yer not takin' me over"!

"Bloody little they'll take over when the military arrives".

> PEARSE

The response was pathetic, a few feeble cheers and a chilling silence. They looked at us as if we were insane: madmen dressed up in silly general's uniforms playing at toy soldier. Thank God Connolly was with me. He looked up at the flags and quietly said, "Isn't it grand?" Then he turned to me, took my hand and shook it firmly. "Thanks be to God, Pearse, that we've lived to see this day". I did manage a slight smile but this was not quite the reception I had imagined. As they drifted away, we posted copies of the proclamation on the front of the G P O and went back inside. There would be no time for self-indulgent thought. Too much remained to be done...

. . . Like barricading Lower Abbey Street to protect the

G.P.O. A squad of men pushed massive rolls of newsprint into the streets. They had commandeered the paper from *The Irish Times* warehouse, by the authority of the Irish Republic. When the paper was in place, they added furniture, machinery, garbage, even bicycles from Keating's bicycle shop.

VOICE-OVER
Jaysus, isn't that a lovely bike?

Would you look at the bloody eejits, throwing it away.

PEARSE
But before the men could finish, a young lad darted out of the crowd, grabbed a bicycle and made off with it. Well the rest of them thought this was a grand idea. So they rushed forward to grab what they could.

(Soundtrack: shots)

We had to fire a few shots, over their heads of course, to keep the barricade from disappearing totally.

(Move centre.)

Here in O'Connell Street, the crowd was growing to alarming proportions. No police were in sight and several members of the clergy were worried about what might happen so the priests decided to take action and disperse the mob themselves. Their strategy was simple. (Pearse moves upstage centre) They linked hands and formed an unbroken picket line, a black, clerical wall, stretching from one side of the very wide avenue to the other. Then, counting on the Irish reluctance to show disrespect for the cloth, (moving slowly downstage) they walked from one end of the street to the other, forcing the crowd to fall back and dissolve before them, squeezing into doorways and side streets. The plan worked, (stop) briefly. But before the priests could sweep their way to the top of the street, the crowd would spill back out behind them. (Pearse steps right) So, the priests reversed their picket and swept back down the street. The result was the same. They made one more attempt and failed again. The mob was too overwhelming . . .

VOICE-OVER
Lancers! Lancers! The Lancers are coming!

PEARSE (SR)
Oh, Lord! At the top of O'Connell Street was a troop of British Lancers and right in front of them was a group of Rathfarnam volunteers. They had arrived late and were trying to reach the Post Office. They made it to a side door and pounded. It was locked and we couldn't find the key. Then someone shouted, "Get in here you bloody fools. Through the windows!"

One of the boys running for the window was a former student, Daniel Porter. As he struggled to climb in, another volunteer tripped and his gun fired right into the boy's shoulder. We hauled him in as carefully and as fast as we could. Danny was a particular favourite of mine but there was no time to do anything except drag him out of the way, because the Lancers were still coming.

(Move downstage left).

Backs erect, they approached in columns as straight as their ceremonial lances. Carbines still holstered, heads fixed high, they acknowledged no one, neither the rabble nor the volunteers fleeing to safety in front of them. They had not been sent to acknowledge. The function of British lancers was to be acknowledged. The entire street was their parade ground and anyone within view was to recognize that they were the British Empire on parade.

(Slide SR - Lancer column)

About one hundred yards north of us, the troop broke columns smartly, fanned out across the street and came to a halt. As the jingle of their trappings ceased, a deep silence fell over the whole street.

VOICE-OVER
Look out fer yerselves! The Sinn Feiners will mow you down!

PEARSE
No Lancer even turned his head at this shouted warning. One of the horses lifted a front hoof, clopped it onto the pavement.

(Pearse raises a foot and clops it down.)

Another horse whinnied.

(Soundtrack: horse whinny)
Their colonel looked to the left, to the right at the sandbagged windows in the Post Office. He raised his eyes towards the rooftops, stared at the two new flags. Then he looked past the barricade, reached for his sword, raised it high, and gave the command.

(Slide SL - Charge)

VOICE-OVER (Colonel, sound of horses hooves)

Charge!

PEARSE

The Lancers, in formation, charged forward.

(Pearse moves upstage.)

Inside the Post Office and on the roof, shouting and confusion gave way to a fearful silence. Forty riflemen, their barrels resting on the ledges, began to realize that this revolution to which they had pledged their lives was fast approaching the moment when they must fire real bullets into real human flesh.

On the upper floor, The O'Rahilly spread the word not to fire until they heard the command. On the ground floor, Connolly spread the same word. Now the approaching Lancers were in full view of the men on the roof. Eager to fire, they still admired the advancing horsemen. They must have known they were in our sights, yet on they came. Now they had reached Nelson's Pillar, just opposite the Henry Street corner. Our plan was to let them come even farther and put them under every gun in the building. But just as the troop passed the pillar, someone lost patience.

(Soundtrack: shot...shot...shots)

A shot rang out. Then another, then a ragged volley of shots. They didn't wait for a command.

(Slides   SR - A shot rang out.   SL -
Volley 1   SR - Volley 2   SL - Volley 3
SR - Volley 4   SL - Dead Horse

SR - Dead Horse   [rapid sequence])

Four Lancers toppled from their saddles, three of them dead as they hit the ground, the fourth wounded. A wave of shock swept over that proud troop as if every man in it had been hit. They broke ranks and what had been a precisely disciplined unit became a milling mass of horses and men, bunched together, totally at our mercy. (Slide sequence finishes.) As the horse of one of the dead Lancers pushed its nose against its master's lifeless body, another ragged volley rang out from both sides of the street and the horse fell dead on top of the man's body. By some miracle of chance, at that moment, our guns became either more merciful or less accurate than anyone could have imagined. Another horse fell, but no more Lancers were hit. Then their Colonel gave an abrupt order to retreat and they galloped off in the direction from which they had come. Even the wounded Lancer hobbled off on foot to safety.

(Move centre.)

When we fully realized what had happened a cheer burst forth as if we had routed the entire British army.

(Point left.)

One man, watching the Lancers retreat, shouted, "Look, it's the Leopardstown races!" I thought to myself, "If that's the way they attack a fortified building, there's hope for us yet."

(Move right.)

But later, as I watched the three dead bodies and the wounded Lancer being taken away by ambulance, I knew exactly what would happen. The full wrath of the British Empire would now descend on us.

(Pearse gets some grenades from the chest.)

So our preparations gained an added momentum. The wounded, including Danny, were looked after immediately. He had only received a flesh wound, thank God, but I gave orders that he was to remain out of harm's way (move centre). The roof was reinforced, barricades were erected at the Prince's Street gate and more supplies were brought in as quickly as possible. Bread, milk, bedding, bandages, everything requisitioned from local merchants. And for every item we took, that merchant was issued a receipt, payable by the government of the Irish Republic. Most people simply felt they were being robbed.

(Pearse crosses to the table and takes out a homemade grenade.)

We also had a number of weapons and explosives that had to be checked. It seemed that everyone was oversupplied with homemade grenades and undersupplied with decent guns or rifles. One man, Lieutenant Liam Clarke, actually proved that the grenades worked. Unfortunately, he was holding it at the time. When the blood was wiped away, we saw that he had suffered little more than light facial wounds which prompted one of the men to express a new concern. "Well if it didn't blow Liam's head off, the divil little use it is to us then."

Every few minutes now, dispatch riders were arriving on their motorcycles, delivering message upon message.

(Pearse picks up a pile of dispatches and

reads.)

Dublin Castle: a guard was shot in a hit and run attack.

St. Stephen's Green: a detachment under Michael Mallin and Countess Constance Markieviez is in charge of the park and prepared for attack from all sides. Now that worries me. The Shelbourne Hotel overlooks the park and they were to have secured it too.

At the Four Courts, Edward Daly's men encountered another troop of Lancers, killing two and driving the rest back. Not a good day for the Lancers.

At the South Dublin Union, Eamonn Ceannt, a schoolteacher, and forty-two men are desperately defending the fifty-two acre workhouse. Less than one man per acre.

Reports were coming in so rapidly now that it was difficult to distinguish them from the rumours, which were coming in even more rapidly. One officer sent in so many messages that Connolly, out of frustration, finally said, "If that man were standing on his right foot, he would send me a dispatch that he planned shortly to put down his left foot."

Outside the mob was getting worse and so was the problem of managing it. The entire Dublin Metropolitan Police Force had been withdrawn from duty and the crowds were pouring out of the slums. They came to stare into the shop windows ... at the expensive clothes, the jewelry, the liquors – hundreds of beautiful items they had only dreamed of owning.

(Slide SL - store fronts   Slide SR -

advertisement)

And without a policeman in sight, what was to prevent them from owning such things now?

The first window to shatter was Noblett's candy store. Shawlies and street urchins jostled and grabbed for the piles of spilling candy, cutting themselves on the broken glass. They snatched pieces of chocolate, mints, fruit drops, Turkish delight ... all splattered with drops of red blood...and still they ate them. Then an old drunk shouted, "They're raiding Nobletts," and the cry echoed down the street. The stampede to reach this fountain of free candy was so frantic that lives were in danger. People cried out in panic as they were squeezed helplessly against each other and against the sides of the buildings, scarcely able to breathe.

The other shops went just as quickly. Drunkards paraded around in silk top hats piled one on top of the other. Women raised their skirts over unwashed legs to enjoy the first silk stockings they had ever worn. Two women fought viciously over a large box of shoes but the woman who prevailed won a strange prize indeed, twelve shoes, all for the same foot. But the grand prize for looting has to go to Winnie O'Byrne and her daughter Agnes.

      (Pearse picks up list of stolen goods and
      reads.)

They were caught with the following items: ... eight window curtains, one pillow, two whalebone corsets, one piece of flannelette, one quilt, one topcoat, two ladies' coats, a half-dozen ladies' hats, four chairs, and two horse hair mattresses.

(He puts the list down and sits.)

We watched this unfolding scene, first in disbelief and then in horror. Was it possible that so many people could shamelessly show themselves to be such a disgrace to Ireland?

Right in front of the Post Office, one woman squatted on the rump of one of the dead horses acting as if it were a chair fit for a queen. Wrapped in a new feather boa and drinking stolen gin, she sang songs ... the like of which I cannot repeat in mixed company.

Sean MacDermott was so offended that he limped into the crowd to plead with them. They just laughed at him. So, The O'Rahilly ordered his men to throw buckets of water on them. Then Connolly said, "Unless we shoot a few of them, you'll never stop them." Since we couldn't do that, there was no solution but to let the rioting run its course.

(Pearse steps forward)

It has been suggested that we leaders care less about the poor and suffering than we do about our own poetry. That is simply not true. I care for all. My whole life has been a slow but certain development towards an awareness of compassion, the ability to feel and share the pain of others and, most important, to attempt to relieve that pain. Believe me when I say that I genuinely care for each of God's creatures. Each of us has our own special ability and that ability must be used where it will do the most good. That is why my school, St. Enda's, has been an overriding passion. And that is why Ireland is an overriding passion.

(Soundtrack: music: *The Women of Ireland*, Pan Pipes)

I do care for these people and I know precisely the terrible conditions from which they come. Look.

(Lights dim, music continues. Slide show of Dublin's poor:

	SL - poor 1
SR - poor 2	SL - poor 3
SR - poor 4	SL - poor 5
SR - poor 6	SL - poor 7
SR - poor 8	SL - poor 9
SR - poor 10	SL - poor 11
SR - poor 12	SL - poor 13
SR - poor 14	SL - poor 15
SR - poor 16	SL - poor 17
SR - poor 18	SL - poor 19
SR - poor 20	SL - poor 21
SR - poor 22	SL - poor 23

Pearse moves far SL and watches the slides.)

VOICE-OVER (Pearse)

My instinct is with the landless man against the lord of lords, and with the breadless man against the master of millions...I calculate that one third of the people of Dublin are underfed, that half the children attending Irish primary schools are ill-nourished. Inspectors of the National Board will tell you that there is no use in visiting primary schools in Ireland after one or two in the afternoon; the children are too weak and drowsy with hunger to be capable of answering intelligently. I suppose there are twenty thousand families in Dublin in whose domestic economy milk and butter are all but unknown; black tea and dry bread are their staple articles of diet. There are many thousand fireless hearthplaces in Dublin on the bitterest days of winter...Twenty thousand families live in one-room tenements. It is common to find two or three families occupying the same room; and sometimes one of the families will have a lodger! We must find a way to enrich their meagre lives. We must!

(Music and slides finish.)

PEARSE

As much as I hate what they do now, I can't blame them. They are the result and not the cause. I pray with all my heart that what we do here will one day improve the lives of all the people in Ireland.

(Lights return to full. Pearse moves forward)

Despite the chaos outside, a semblance of order was beginning to emerge inside the Post Office. A munitions section was set up to inspect and adjust the rifles, so we could shoot the British instead of each other, and best of all, the women's branch had arrived, the Cumann na mBan.

(Slide SR - Cumann na mBan)

They quickly organized the hospital and commissary where much help was needed.

And while we worked, a variety of visitors came and went.

(Slide SL - Francis Sheehy-Skeffington)

One of them, Francis Sheehy-Skeffington, was a well-known pacifist. He was extremely concerned about the looting but he had no alternatives to offer us, so rather than do nothing, he went back out into the streets and tried to reason with the crowds. It was not an effective method.

After that, The O'Rahilly's sister, Anna, came into the Post office. Like my sister, Mary Brigid, she wanted him to leave. When he refused, she marched over to me, grabbed me by the arm and said fiercely, "This is all your fault you know," and stormed out. Does every sister in Ireland plan to seize my arm and reprimand me? I...

> (Soundtrack: fireworks
> [simultaneous]
> Slides SR - Fireworks 1   SL - Fireworks 2
> SR - Fireworks 3
> SL - Fireworks 4)

Some children had found a huge batch of fireworks and ignited them. Skyrockets, Roman candles, star showers - more spectacular than all the gunfire of the Rising. Soon the boot shop was in flames and the fire brigade had to come and rescue the men, women, and children who lived above the store. One woman was actually about to give birth and under no circumstances was she going to leave her bed. Finally, the firemen carried her, kicking and screaming, downstairs to safety. And in the midst of all this, Father John Flannagan arrived to hear confession. We gave him a room at the rear of the Post Office and he was kept busy until 11:30 at night. I wanted everyone to be spiritually prepared for the very real possibility of death.

Outside in the streets the scene looked unreal. No tram

cars. Silent spectators huddled in front of a burning building. Two dead horses rotting on the pavement. The street littered with empty bottles and stolen merchandise that didn't come up to the standards of the looters. It was a sad sight.

My thoughts were interrupted by James Connolly who was in a much more expansive mood than I was. As this first day of the Rising drew to a close he pointed out our accomplishments. The Republic had been declared. Irish soldiers occupied so many parts of the city that it might be said we controlled Dublin. And, in every encounter with British troops, we had come off victorious. Then Connolly pulled a dispatch from his pocket and handed it to me.

(Pearse picks up dispatch from the table and reads.)

"The Citizen Army has captured King George and Lord Kitchener...in the Henry Street wax museum.

We immediately gave orders for the wax figures to be brought here to headquarters. (Return dispatch.) What will the British think when they see a king and an English lord manning the barricades alongside Irish rebels?

All in all it is a fine revolution for a day.

(Soundtrack: Music: *The Minstrel Boy*.
Lights fade to black as Pearse exits.)

END OF ACT ONE

EASTER RISING:
THE LAST WORDS OF PATRICK PEARSE

ACT TWO

AT RISE: Slide SR - Easter Rising
                 Slide SL - The Last Words Of Patrick Pearse

Pearse enters as an instrumental version of *Dublin in the Rare Old Times* plays. Lights are full.

Wrapped in a blanket, he sits and sleeps. Lights fade to black.

          (Slide SR - Black and White Rose   SL -
          same B & W   SR - Red Rose   SL -
          same red)

          VOICE-OVER (The Rose Tree)
'O words are lightly spoken,'
Said Pearse to Connolly,
'Maybe a breath of politic words
Has withered our Rose Tree;
Or maybe but a wind that blows

31

Across the bitter sea.'

'It needs to be but watered,'
James Connelly replied,
'To make the green come out again
And spread the blossom from the bud
To be the garden's pride.'

'But where can we draw water,'
Said Pearse to Connolly,
'When all the wells are parched away?
O plain as plain can be
There's nothing but our own red blood
Can make a right Rose Tree.'

> (Full lights. Soundtrack: Machine gun fire
> startles Pearse who goes to a basin, splashes
> water on his face and dries off with a towel.
> Slide SR - Tuesday   Slide SL -April 25)

PEARSE

We were awakened by the sound of machine gun fire in the distance but it posed no immediate threat to headquarters. I don't know how long I had slept but it wasn't long enough.

One of the first visitors to the post office that morning, not surprisingly, was a postman ready to pick up the mail for his route. The sentry barred him with his bayonet and said, "Go home. There's no mail today."

"No mail? Sure, why not? It's Tuesday."

"Because there's a revolution going on. That's why not'"

"Since when is there no mail of a Tuesday?"

"Since yesterday."

"But yesterday was Monday."

Now who could argue with that logic? The sentry raised his bayonet and stepped forward. "You heard me say there was no mail. Now, will you feck off? Go home!" There were no letters delivered that morning.

Meanwhile, the men were trying to eat breakfast. One thing they all agreed on was how bad the
food was. Desmond Fitzgerald, who was helping with the meals, finally lost his patience and snapped at one of the young gripers. "Do you think I'm obliged to serve four course dinners to you, when some of you never had a decent bite in your lives before? Even if you are here to die for Ireland, eat that crust of bread." And he ate it.

After breakfast, I went on to inspect the Earl Street garrison and made sure the snipers were in position. While I did that, the Cumann na mBan smuggled in more guns, concealed within the folds of their long skirts. On my way back I saw something remarkable. In the centre of O'Connell Street a girl with an armful of stolen lingerie began stripping off her clothes, item by item. One man came up to see what was happening, looked and cried out, "Mother of God, she's naked!" Then a drunken, middle-aged woman wearing stolen shoes, a stolen dress, and a stolen hat said, "Would you look at the bloody hoor. Has she got no morality at all?" Another man just stood and sighed, "Ah, if only me own wife had a figure like that!"

There were no police to stop her or anyone else but Francis

Sheehy-Skeffington had a plan. At one o'clock he walked out of the Post Office with a bundle of posters, a paste pot, a brush, and as many walking sticks as he could carry. A crowd quickly gathered to read his message:

(Pearse picks up a poster and reads.)

When there are no regular police on the streets, it becomes the duty of citizens to police the streets themselves and to prevent such spasmodic looting as has taken place...Civilians (men and women) who are willing to co-operate to this end are asked to attend at Westmoreland Chambers at five o'clock this afternoon.

His plan was to form a civilian constabulary that would fight crime with walking sticks...that's right, walking sticks. Sheehy-Skeffington was thought of as a gentle, harmless man, with peculiar ideas and although he may have been a pacifist, he was no coward. Yesterday he walked right through a cross fire of bullets to help a wounded officer who was bleeding to death on the pavement near the castle.

VOICE-OVER
Sir, they've been driven out of the Green!

(Slide SR - Mallin   Slide SL - Countess)

PEARSE
That's what I was afraid of. St. Stephen's green was never to have been fully occupied. Michael Mallin who is in charge is a nineteen-year army veteran and his second in command, Countess Markieviecz, is the highest-ranking woman in the Army of the Republic. Both of them know that the park is indefensible because right beside the green is the tallest building in the area, the Shelbourne Hotel. We

should have controlled it but instead the British are occupying it. Machine gun fire from the upper floors was decimating our troops at the very moment I received this eyewitness account:

(Pearse reads)

"The rain is falling now persistently and from the Shelbourne Hotel snipers are exchanging bullets. Some distance beyond the Shelbourne, a volunteer is stretched out on a seat just within the railings. He is not dead and now and again his hand moves feebly in a gesture for aid. The hand is completely red with blood. His face cannot be seen. He is just a limp mass upon which the rain beats pitilessly and he is sodden and shapeless, and most miserable to see. We cannot draw him in for the spot is covered by snipers. He will have to stay there, in his agony, until the fall of night."

PEARSE

The entire park was vulnerable and after five more men were killed in a hail of bullets, the rest managed to retreat across the street into the College of Surgeons. For the moment, they were safe.

Back here in the Post Office rumours flew faster than the bullets. Just listen to this:

(Pearse reads from the same dispatch pile.)

The Germans have landed troops...A whole fleet of submarines is in Dublin Bay...The British are planning a night airplane attack on the Post Office...and my favourite...Labour leader Jim Larkin is on his way with an army of fifty thousand Irish Americans.

PEARSE

I know the rumours are outrageous but Desmond Fitzgerald begged for answers. He said, "I would like to tell my people the most hopeful thing that is known for certain at this moment. Is there anything to suggest we may get outside help?" I hesitated and said, "Smoke has been seen in the bay. We honestly believe there are submarines."

I lied. I lied because hope is better than despair. We were all acutely aware of the impending attack and nervous. I began to pace anxiously from station to station in the post office but I'm afraid all I accomplished was to make poor Tom Clarke even more upset. "For God's sake, he said, "won't someone find that man an office and get him out of the way?" I stopped pacing and sat there...and waited.

(Slide SR - British troops   Slide SL - more troops.)

At about half past midnight a small but excited group of citizens burst into the Post office and informed us that hundreds of British Soldiers were nearing Parnell Square at the top of O'Connelll Street, just two blocks above us. Connolly dispatched several scouts, and called the Post Office to full alert. The men, half asleep, were shaken awake.

(Lights dim)

Muscles tightened, mouths went dry. Lights were extinguished, all noise was eliminated.
Even so, the sound of praying could still be heard.

(A single spot narrows to Pearse's face.)

VOICE-OVER (The Lord's Prayer, low)

PEARSE

No one doubted that the fight to the finish was about to begin. The British would come on, wave after wave, caring nothing for their losses, which would be enormous. They might eventually win because of their overwhelming numbers, but before they did, they would know the full fury of Irish bravery. At every window two or three riflemen crouched and behind the riflemen, more men, sometimes women, with grenades. Tom Clarke was one of them. He was going to get some of his own back for all those painful, hungry years in British prisons. Through the raindrops, falling softly now, two hundred pairs of eyes peered out, scanning the dimly lit streets,
expecting at any moment to see a wave of onrushing khaki uniforms. Rifle barrels turned toward each sound in the night. And at last, when footsteps were heard on the pavement, the tension was almost explosive. Suddenly, a man, alone, came around the corner and walked toward the Post Office. For a moment his life wasn't worth a farthing. Dozens of guns zeroed in on him. But just in time, I heard:

VOICE-OVER
Hold your fire, boys - it's Sean O'Kelly.

PEARSE

We laughed nervously as little Sean came running into the building. He had been to Parnell Square and found no British there. Another false alarm. How many more times would we be routed out of sleep and sent to the windows to wait, for nothing. But the grumbling didn't last for long. Everyone was too tired. So they stretched out and tried to sleep again. But only a few had managed it before they were sent to the windows one more time. The other scouts had begun returning, all with the same information. This time, the British were coming and they were coming in force.

Again, Connolly called an alert, and again the British took their time. Just out of sight of the Post Office, they stopped to study the situation and deploy their forces. Every sign showed they were preparing to advance any second now. Yet the seconds turned into minutes and the minutes stretched into hours and they did not move. As dawn approached two hundred exasperated, sleepless, red-eyed Volunteers were still staring out the windows of the G P O, waiting... watching for the enemy.

> (Soundtrack: Artillery shells   Lights full.
> Slides: SR - Wednesday   Slides SL -
> April 26.)

Listen to that!

> (Second artillery shell.)

Do you know what that is?

> (Third artillery shell.)

Artillery. British artillery. Only yesterday James Connolly told everyone that artillery was the one weapon the British would not use. He said, "No capitalist government will use artillery and destroy the property of its own capitalist class. They will certainly never shell O'Connell Street." Do you know where those shells are landing? Just a few blocks from here on Liberty Hall. James is a great leader, a great general, but on this particular point, he was wrong.

(Slide SR - the *Helga*)

Through the foggy dew of the morning, a British gunboat sailed up the River Liffey as far as Butt Bridge. It was the *Helga* ...

(Pearse points to screen)

... here to destroy the headquarters of the Irish trade unions and all the rebels who were inside, but, in fact, the building was empty except for the caretaker, Peter Ennis. Peter had to flee for his life. As he began to run, the British turned a machine gun on him. (Pearse steps forward) Bullets hit the pavement in front of him and behind him. They ricocheted off the roadway and the walls of the building along his escape route and still he ran on and on. People held their breath as he careened madly down the street. Will he escape? Yes, yes, he will...No, no, he won't. He..."My God!" someone shouted as he jumped from a bullet that sparked on the pavement right by his toe. A hundred yards in nine seconds. It's a record! No, wait. He does the next hundred yards in five seconds and then disappears into the distance, his breath in his fist, his heart in his mouth - but safe at last. Well done, Peter!

The *Helga* continued shelling until the empty building was demolished. Then she sailed smugly down the Liffey to attack the rear of the Boland's Mills garrison but Eamon de Velara was too smart for them. He ran one of our flags up the flagpole of an abandoned distillery nearby and the *Helga* proceeded to blaze away at another empty building.

Here in the Post Office, unshaven men, and quite a few not yet old enough to shave, peered out the windows along their gun barrels. Danny Porter was one of them. I still worried about him and hoped he would come to no harm.

> VOICE-OVER
>
> Sir!

> PEARSE
>
> Yes, what is it?

> VOICE-OVER
>
> Listen, sir!

> PEARSE
>
> We heard what sounded like a heavy truck approaching from the top of O'Connell Street.

(Slide SL - armoured truck.)

Then I saw it. It was a huge vehicle with an armour protected engine and a cylindrical metal body. Gun barrels protruded from tiny slits and circular holes. We had never seen anything like it. Some of the men fired but it kept on coming. The bullets just bounced off making an almost musical sound as it drew closer by the moment.

One man who had not yet fired at it was a Volunteer named Joseph Sweeney. He studied it carefully, noticing the holes and slits in its armour, and in particular the widest slit, a one-foot by one inch opening in the front of the body. It seemed reasonable to Sweeney that the driver would be just behind that slit. Raising his rifle, he trained his eye on the narrow opening and fired, once, twice, three times. Each time, his bullet struck armour and the vehicle continued to roll forward. He took aim again and fired a fourth time. This time there was no sound of impact against metal. The bullet went neatly through the slit. The vehicle rolled a few feet closer, its engine coughed, and it chugged to a stop. After a few more shots at it, we held our fire, watching, wondering breathlessly whether it would start again. After several minutes, we looked at each other and smiled. The iron monster was dead in the street.

Security was tightened here at the Post Office and strangers were no longer allowed into the building in case they were spies. One eager, young volunteer decided to venture outside the building to look for a few. He returned shortly with a very proper dignified looking gentleman and marched him in at gunpoint. "I've caught a spy," he announced proudly. The gentleman was furious. He turned red and sputtered, scarcely able to form a word. I said, "What makes you think he's a spy?" The volunteer replied, "He's a British Officer."

"How do you know?"

A silly grin lit his face. "Because when I said, 'Quick march,' he started off on the left foot."

"Right." I thanked the volunteer and quickly took the gentleman aside. You see, he was the headmaster of a local military academy for young boys. Of course he knew how to march and, of course, I owed him an apology.

After I had escorted the poor fellow safely to the door, Connolly informed me that Brennan- Whitmore and his men had taken the Imperial Hotel, directly across the street but they were unable to communicate with us. The bullet-swept street made it impossible for anyone to carry a dispatch across to headquarters. Then Brennan-Whitmore thought of a solution. While one man held the end of a ball of twine, another man threw the ball across O'Connell Street to the Post Office where it was wound around a post and thrown back.

(Pearse holds up a can)

Then a pail was fastened to the twine as a message carrier and we had a two-way "telegraph" system. The invention had only one flaw. As the pail moved slowly across the street, it became a very attractive target for British marksmen. See what I mean.

(Soundtrack: rifle shot. Pearse puts a finger in the bullet hole. More shots.)

We managed two more trips, but by the third trip, it looked like this.

(Pearse picks up a splayed can.)

When Brennan Whitmore saw one of his men fastening a new pail to the twine, he grabbed it and shouted, "For God's sake, man, just tie the message to the twine. They'll never see a bit of paper."

(Pearse unfolds a paper to reveal a bullet hole.)

Well, some got through, in a manner of speaking.
When evening arrived, the gunfire seemed to slacken. (Gentle) As I looked round at the men and women, I became convinced that they would all perish in this Rising and I had brought them here. Now I make no attempt to

deny responsibility for the death and destruction of the Rising. The only question is this: how will it appear in the eyes of God? We are, after all, waging a war, and the church has never forbidden war so long as it is fought for a worthy cause. Can anyone doubt that the freedom of Ireland is a worthy cause? We are fighting for our lives and we are willing to die, if need be, as a sacrifice to that cause.

We are willing to die as thousands before us have died. When Cromwell came to Ireland his aim was the complete extermination of the Irish people. His Puritan ministers charged the English army to, and I quote, "to kill all that were, young man and old, children and maiden". They swept across Ireland like the plague.

We are willing to die as millions did during the famine years of Queen Victoria. During her reign alone, one and a quarter million people starved to death when the potato crops failed. Entire families died in the fields with their mouths green from eating grass. Sometimes a child survived, but it is said, not totally in jest, that you can count all the orphans who survived the great hunger, on one set of fingers and toes, and still have three fingers and a toe left over. Three and a half million were evicted from houses they or their fathers had built. All in all, over four million people were forced to flee the country they loved.

More and more, I realised that Ireland could rely only on force, in some form or another, because everything else had failed. Irishmen were simply struggling to keep alive and England deemed it a crime. Surely the people of Ireland deserve redemption after centuries of bondage. If some of us must die to achieve this redemption, so be it. Our purpose is to restore life to Ireland and if the resurrection of Ireland results from this Rising, from the sacrifice of our lives, we will have succeeded.

(Soundtrack: shots)

Outside, bullets splattered against the walls, no more than twenty feet away. Fires were beginning to spread through the abandoned buildings on Lower Abbey Street. By this time everyone had abandoned the myth of a possible victory. Here, in the Post Office, James Connolly walked around looking into the faces of each that he passed, exhausted, frightened faces. Then, without comment, he stood quietly and began to sing. It was, *The Soldiers' Song*, one of their favourite marching tunes.

(Soundtrack: *The Soldiers' Song*)

As people mellowed and began to listen, a report was handed to me (music fades) which destroyed any joy that I might have felt from the song. Francis Sheehy-Skeffington had been murdered . . . murdered by an Irishman, a mad officer in the Royal Irish Rifles, Captain J. C. Bowen-Colthurst. Last night, Skeffington was arrested and at approximately 10:30 this morning, without any warning, Colthurst took him out of his cell and ordered his men to shoot him. Four soldiers fired again and again and again until his lifeless body was riddled with bullets. This gentle, innocent victim died without a word of explanation, with only the memory of a mad rampage from the night before.

He was first questioned at Portobello Barracks where Colthurst stormed in and said, "You are to be executed".

"What are the charges?" asked Skeffington.

"Charges? Don't you know that a state of emergency has

been declared, that we have special powers?"

"But I've done nothing wrong, I'm a pacifist."

Colthurst's eyes glazed over, " 'Who so sheddeth a man's blood, by man shall his blood be shed.' I'm Irish you know and it's a terrible thing to have to shoot one's own countrymen. Don't you agree? A terrible thing, but a necessity."

"You can't do this to innocent people."

"You are now in my custody. I think you had better say your prayers."

"Most certainly not."

"What?"

"I refuse."

"Kneel down! Kneel! I said, kneel!" And they knocked him down and again Colthurst prayed.

"Oh Lord God, if it should please thee to take away the life of this man, forgive him for our Lord, Jesus Christ's sake. Amen."

"Do you mean to shoot me?"

"Listen Skeffington, you will accompany me on patrol as a hostage. If there's trouble from anyone, if we're sniped at from any quarter, you will be shot at once."

And so they began their bloody journey. As they passed

Rathmines Church, three, innocent boys were stopped. Colthurst snapped at them.

"And where might you be coming from at this time of the evening? Speak up!"

One boy, a terrified youngster barely in his teens, muttered, " A meeting sir, in the church."

"Don't you know that Marshall Law has been declared, that I could have you shot like dogs?"

Then he turned to one of his soldiers and commanded, "Bash him!" The soldier raised the butt of his rifle and smashed it into the boy's jaw, breaking it. As they tried to run away, Colthurst removed his gun from his holster and shot the injured boy in the back. Skeffington broke free and ran to the boy. "He's not dead," he cried and tried to shield the boy with his body. Colthurst stepped forward. Calmly and coolly, he kicked Skeffington out of the way. The boy, lying in a pool of blood, moaned one last time. Colthurst raised his revolver, cocked the hammer, and ...

(Blackout. A single shot is fired.)

END OF ACT TWO

EASTER RISING:
THE LAST WORDS OF PATRICK PEARSE

ACT THREE

AT RISE: Slide SR - *Easter Rising*
Slide SL - *The Last Words Of Patrick Pearse* The song, *The Foggy Dew*, plays. Stage lights are on low. House lights go out when the song reaches the words "Angelus bell". A slide sequence, showing the destruction of Dublin, begins:

SR - Thursday, SL - April 27 SR - Foggy Dew 1 through SL - Foggy Dew 42 SR - Foggy Dew 43 SL - Foggy Dew 43

(Slide 43 is the only colour slide and ends the sequence with the same bright red "Fire" on both screens.)

> Pearse enters quietly at the beginning of
> the sequence and stands between the
> two screens facing upstage. Lights go to
> black. At the end of the song and slide
> sequence, the lights come up on Pearse.
> He turns and recites *The Rebel*.

PEARSE

I am come of the seed of the people, the people that
    sorrow,
That have no treasure but hope,
No riches laid up but a memory
Of an Ancient glory.
My mother bore me in bondage, in bondage my
    mother was born,
I am of the blood of serfs;
The children with whom I have played, the men and
    women with whom I have eaten,
Have had masters over them, have been under the
    lash of masters,
And, though gentle, have served churls;
And now I speak, being full of vision;
I speak to my people, and I speak in my people's name
    To the masters of my people.
I say to my people that they are holy, that they are
    August, despite their chains,
That they are greater than those that hold them, and
    stronger and purer,
That they have but need of courage, and to call on the
name of their God,
God the unforgetting, the dear God that loves the
    peoples

For whom He died naked, suffering shame.

And I say to my people's masters: Beware,

Beware of the thing that is coming, beware of the risen
people,

Who shall take what ye would not give. Did ye think to
conquer the people,

Or that Law is stronger than life and than men's
desire to be free?

We will try it out with you, ye that have harried and
held,

Ye that have bullied and bribed, tyrants, hypocrites,
liars!

> (Slide SR - Foggy Dew 44   Slide SL -
> Foggy Dew 44 repeat   Both slides show
> the same fire scene in black and white.
> Pearse points to the screens.)

That was the first time it had happened since Moscow
- the first time a capital city has been burned in over a
century.

Outside, the putrid stench of the two rotting horse
carcasses filled the air. Because the windows had been
smashed, it was impossible to shut out the odour.
Several of the men became nauseated and vomited
their breakfast, which was a shame because the
Cumann na mBan had the commissary running as
smoothly as a restaurant and the food was finally
decent.

By 11 A.M., the flames were only a block away from

the Post Office and the British infantry was getting closer all the time. Our boys were firing at them so fast and so often that their rifles became too hot to touch and one after another, they jammed. One of the women solved that problem. She appeared with a garbage container filled with tin cans, sardine cans. They drained the oil that was left in each can and when they had enough they poured it onto the guns. In no time at all they were firing again. A fishy solution, but effective.

Unfortunately, a few of the men were beginning to show the effects of the constantly increasing pressure and lack of sleep. One Volunteer began running through the building shouting and waving his gun madly. I rushed over and tried to calm him but it was useless. He threw the rifle down and screamed his way out into the street. Before he had gone twenty feet, a bullet hit him, spun him around, and threw him to the ground, As he lie there, writhing on the pavement, calling out in pain, I felt completely and utterly helpless, as if a part of me were dying with him.

While two hospital men went out under a Red Cross flag to drag him back, Connolly decided that we needed to shore up our position and led a group of men to build a barricade right here in Prince's Street. As he supervised the work, he warned everybody to stay under cover and then promptly proceeded to ignore his own advice. No one even noticed him grimace after the sound of a rifle shot. He simply said he'd be back directly and marched into the Post Office. Behind a folding screen in the hospital section he bared his arm and Jim Ryan, who was in charge, dressed what was only a flesh wound. "Not a word about this to anyone," he said and marched back out to the barricades. After inspecting the work and releasing the men, he started back again. He had taken no more than a step or two when a bullet hit the pavement, skipped up, and shattered his left ankle. Connolly went down as if someone had hit him with a sledgehammer. But he knew he had to get back. On his hands and one knee he dragged himself along, barely conscious with the pain and the nausea, until he collapsed in the gutter. Fortunately one of his men saw him and he was carried back inside.

We had captured a British Army doctor, Lieutenant Mahoney, and he examined the mess of bone fragments that had been an ankle. Connolly was losing blood so he applied a tourniquet while an assistant fashioned a splint. There was nothing to hold the torn ankle in place. Pieces of bone were protruding right through the flesh. And there was no anesthetic, only a weak solution of chloroform. As Jim Ryan administered it, Mahoney released the tourniquet, extracted the bits of bone fragment, tied off the blood vessels, and attached a new splint with a special foot piece.   Throughout all this, Connolly remained conscious. Mercifully, we managed to find some morphine later and he was able to sleep through the heat which increased constantly through the night. Men were falling everywhere from heat prostration. Coughing and choking from the smoky air, they hosed each other down as well as the window casements which were so hot they produced instant steam.

As the night passed into day, I stared at an enormous fire across the street. The walls of one of the buildings cracked, wavered and then crashed, thundering down, pieces of red hot brick smashing onto the street. The city that I loved was crumbling around me.

(Slides: SR - Friday. Slide: SL - April 28)

The next day went by in a blaze, and I do mean in a blaze. Only two blocks of twisted, smoldering steel and the jagged remnants of brick walls remained. Yet we had only been hit twice. Obviously the British were saving the best for last.

By mid-morning, we had just finished removing the last of the grenades and explosives from the roof where the first incendiary bomb had landed. Prisoners were taken from there to the cellar where we hoped they would be safe, then, I gathered the women together and tried to tell them they were to be evacuated. For a moment, they were still, then I thought there was going to be another revolution. "No," they shouted. "We won't go. We stay as long as the men stay!" Well I lost every last bit of calm and poise that I had. I never did have a way with women but I tried to tell them that although they might be killed out there, if they stayed here, the British would kill them for sure and what use would they be to Ireland then? Reluctantly, they accepted my argument and marched off under the protection of a Red Cross flag.

(Slide SR - Fire hose in the GPO.)

By mid-afternoon, flames were everywhere and the hoses were breaking down. They produced more profanity than water. Most of them were so old and rotten that the water leaked out before even reaching the nozzles. The best we could do was to try and keep the fire away from the elevator shaft. If the flames went down there where the explosives were stored, our Rising would end with a climax more spectacular than anything Dublin had ever seen.

(Soundtrack: Overlapping *Hail Mary/
Our Father*

Slide SL - Priest in GPO)

Behind the noise of crackling wood and roaring flame you could hear the constant sound of praying.

Flames leaped and curled everywhere, especially around the glass canopy that covered the central court. Red-hot embers blew down from the roof and landed all around us. There were so many fires that it was impossible to control them. And now we had to face the truth. We had to evacuate and we couldn't wait until dark. We had to leave as soon as possible and we had to take James Connolly with us.

So the O'Rahilly went ahead with a special squad to secure a new headquarters. While the rest of us waited, I asked James if he thought he could stand the move if we carried him on his stretcher. "Carry me on a stretcher?' he said. "Why this sounds like revolution deluxe. You walk and I ride, it's grand". His humour and his courage were an inspiration to everyone. Finally, it was as dark as it was going to get. I went to the prisoners, shook their hands, apologized for any suffering they had endured, and told them they were now free to make a break for it. I only hoped their own snipers could recognize another British uniform in the darkness.

At 8:40 P.M. I spoke to the men. "I want all of you to be ready to go out and face the machine guns as if you were on parade." And they did. Along with Joseph Plunkett and Sean MacDermott, I stood out in the street and spurred the men on. It was a choice...between flames or bullets. Close by, young Danny Porter had decided that he would use his own body to shield me from any possible injury. He seemed oblivious to the bullets that landed all around us. "Don't worry, sir," he shouted." I'll get you through, safe and . . .

(Soundtrack: a single shot.

Slide SR - Boy as Cu Chulainn   Slide

SL - Warrior Cu Chulainn)

And he fell in a heap at my feet, this boy who had studied under me, who had boarded at my school, this young warrior who had fought at my side. While the others continued the evacuation, we carried him back inside. He was barely breathing. As I knelt over him, he leaned up as if he wanted to say something. He looked at me with big, brown eyes...innocent, child eyes and he said, "We haven't failed, have we, sir?" "No Danny, we haven't failed." And then the air seemed to go out of him and he was still. I reached out, slowly, and placed my hand on his heart. Suddenly, he grabbed my arm and took one great gasp of air. His eyes were open wide and he looked into me, right inside my soul. Then he sank back down and his eyes closed. I felt for a pulse. There was none.

As I raised his lifeless body, and held him for a moment, I knew that I had killed him as surely as if I had pulled the trigger myself. Danny had been a fine student, but more than anything, he loved the plays. I remember him dressed like Cu Chulainn, dressed like a warrior, and I remember the words he recited, "I care not though I were to live one day and one night, if only my fame and deeds live after me."

I held him, with his head resting on my shoulder and I began to pray. I prayed for life. "Dear God, I beg of you, trade my life for his. He is too young. Take me and return the boy. Live. Please. I beg of you. Live."... And then I felt something move. He was breathing. He was breathing and he was alive!

(Pearse rises.)

I believe that at that very moment a miracle had happened...We placed Danny on a stretcher and he was removed along with James Connolly. He had made enough of a sacrifice.

(Pearse starts to wave, stops and continues.)

To the best of my knowledge, the Post Office was empty now but I had to be sure so I went back in to look for stragglers . . .

(Pearse moves about the stage as if he is looking for people.)

I quickly made the rounds but found no one, only some dispatches that had been left behind. Although I was certain they would not survive, I didn't want the British to have them, so I lit a match and destroyed them myself. As I stood there, surrounded by flames, I knew how the captain of the *Titanic* must have felt. We had set sail on a particular course and the outcome was totally evident. There was no choice but to move inexorably to our deadly conclusion.

And I wondered, what would I leave behind? Would I be a hero or just another sad, frustrated failure making one final, passionate gesture? Oh, I know what some of the men say about me, that I'm nothing but a fat, balding, pedantic, old schoolmaster, who also writes bad poetry. Even Sean MacDermott calls me pop - P.O.P. - That's short for "poor old Pearse". At least he means it affectionately, I hope. In my heart, I know that I have squandered the splendid years of my youth. I have closed my heart to women and chosen another way. And I know that, given the chance, I will still squander those years. I can only pray, pray as I did in a poem, that I have made the right decision:

O wise men, riddle me this: what if the dream come
     true?
What if the dream come true? And if millions unborn
     shall dwell
In the house that I shaped in my heart, the noble
     house of my thought?
Lord, I have staked my soul, I have staked the lives of
     my kin
On the truth of Thy dreadful word. Do not remember
     my failures,
But remember this my faith.

VOICE-OVER
Pearse, for God's sake get out of there!

> (Slide SR - GPO in flames   Slide SL -
> same)

PEARSE
Time to go. Time to say farewell to a grand building,
the first headquarters of the Irish Republic.

(Pearse salutes.)

I raced out as fast as I could. My eyes were swollen and watery from the heat and smoke, but I made my way up Moore Street where the advance guard had fought their way to a small cottage near the corner of Henry Lane. One of the men went to the cottage door and tried it. It was locked. He decided to open it by shooting the lock.

Inside the cottage were Mr. and Mrs. Thomas McKane, their ten children and Mrs McKane's brother. For two days they had all been confined to this tiny cottage by the gunfire in the area. McKane, with a pair of children in his arms, heard someone try the lock at the back door and went to investigate. He squeezed his way between several of his other children, including his sixteen-year-old daughter, Bridget. Just as McKane reached the door, the Volunteer fired into the lock. The bullet passed through the door, through McKane's shoulder and into Bridget's head. McKane collapsed to the floor still holding the two uninjured children as blood poured from his shoulder. Bridget swooned onto a bed with a hole in the right side of her head. Young Bridget McKane was dead.

We comforted Mrs. McKane as much as we could. We even offered to punish the offending soldier. Incredibly, she just shook her head and said, "Ah, it was only an accident". Then she ran off to get a priest for her husband.

When the priest arrived, Father McInerney, he just stood there staring in disbelief at the bleeding and dead crowded on the floor all around him, soldiers and civilians. He was so overcome that he burst into tears but when he noticed everyone staring at him, he quickly pulled himself together and began going from man to man to administer the last sacraments.

Connolly, sick as he was, called Mrs. McKane over to him and reached out to take her hand. "You're a brave woman," he said, but his words were little consolation for the damage we had just inflicted.

Still, we had to find a way to move on. One of the McKane daughters, Mary, suggested that we should knock holes in the houses and move on up the street that way. Since the houses were connected, we could move through the inner walls without being seen. It was the obvious thing to do and the men set to work. Eventually they would make it to Kelly's Market at the corner of Sackville Lane.

My brother, Willie, and I, stretched out on a table and tried to sleep but the sounds of gunfire and artillery made it impossible, so I got up, went downstairs, and began crawling through the holes, from house to house, making sure the men were as comfortable as possible.

(Soundtrack: huge explosion)

At 3 AM, the fires in the Post Office had finally reached the stored gunpowder and gelignite. The explosion rocked the entire area for several blocks and made sure that no one slept.

(Slides: SR - Saturday   SL - April 29)

With morning came the realization that we were completely destitute of medical supplies. There was little or no water and we had already used every spare sheet to replace the blood soaked bandages. We were also dangerously low on food. When I found a sack of wheat meal in one of the houses and gave it to Elizabeth O'Farrell, I thought she might make some bread with it. She was polite enough to accept it without pointing out that they had none of the other necessary ingredients.

After a semblance of breakfast, we moved on up the street to Hanlon's Fish Market. It was here that news of The O'Rahilly reached me. The men posted at the windows of Kelly's Market had seen him in the street. He was sprawled on the pavement and obviously dead. Blood was spattered on his green officer's uniform and a few feet from his body lay his felt hat, his revolver, and the bodies of two of his men.

(Soundtrack: "Help. Help. For the love of God, Help us".)

Outside, the commotion was frightening. Three

civilians waving white flags and shouting were trying to run across the street to escape a fire on the other side. "Don't shoot!" I shouted, hoping the British would give the same order, but they didn't. Two volleys of bullets riddled the three men. As I looked out at the bodies, one of them quivered and spurted blood. I raised my hand for silence. "Listen, I want everyone to hear this. There is to be no more firing until further notice. That's an order. Now pass it along".

Until now, I had been ready to storm the barricades one more time. But not now. This was the moment when I knew it had to end.

After a brief conference with MacDermott and Connolly, we asked Elizabeth O'Farrell if she could find us a white flag. Michael O'Reilly reached into his breast pocket and pulled out a large white handkerchief that hadn't been laundered for a week.

> (Pearse takes out a handkerchief and attaches it to a stick.)

Remembering what had just happened to the three civilians, Michael put the flag on a stick and stuck it out the door.

> (Soundtrack: shots)

As we expected, a volley of bullets made him pull it back in. Then he stuck it out again...but this time they recognized it and no one fired.

(Slide SR - Elizabeth O'Farrell)

At forty-five minutes past noon, I handed the flag to Elizabeth O'Farrell. I took her hand and said, "God be with you, Elizabeth". Then she stepped out into the street. She was to make her way to the British lines and ask to speak to the commanding general. Walking slowly and deliberately, she approached the barricade where several guns pointed directly towards her. Then she spoke. "The Commandant of the Irish Republican Army wishes to treat with the Commandant of the British Forces in Ireland. A colonel replied, "The Sinn Feiners, you mean". Then he turned to one of his soldiers and said, "Take that Red Cross patch off her uniform. Bring her over there and search her. She's a spy". When they searched her, they found two pairs of scissors, some candy, a slice of bread, and three small cakes. Having decided that she was not dangerous, they left her waiting in Tom Clarke's tobacco shop. Eventually, a tall, slender general appeared in the doorway. He was Brigadier General W. H. M. Lowe, commander of the Dublin forces. After considering her message, he said to her, "I have a motor car outside. I shall take you to the barricade at the top of Moore Street. You will return to Mr. Pearse and tell him that General Lowe will not treat at all until he surrenders unconditionally. You will also tell him that you must be back here in a half-hour, and that in the meantime, hostilities must go on".

When Elizabeth returned with the information, I wrote a reply saying that I wanted no terms for myself but I did want to know how the men would be treated. The response was short and clear.
I must surrender unconditionally and I had a half hour to do it.

At 2:20 PM, I concluded my final meeting with Clarke, Connolly, MacDermott, and Plunkett. I tried to make myself as presentable as possible. Although my uniform was soiled, I wiped my boots and brushed my hat as well as I could. With Elizabeth at my side, we stepped out into the street. I held my head up and walked as proudly as possible. Just past Kelly's, I saw for the first time, the body of The O'Rahilly. He was naked. Every stitch of clothing, every piece of his uniform was gone, stolen. In the pocket of my coat was the last remaining tricolor flag. I opened it and draped it over his body. There wasn't even time for a prayer. Our half-hour was running out.

> (Pearse salutes.   Slide SL - Surrender photo)

By 2:30, I stood face to face with General Lowe. I removed my sword and, using the accepted ceremony, offered it, in both hands, palms upward. He took it, handed it to an aide and said:

"My only concession is that I will allow the other commandants to surrender. I understand you have the Countess Markiewiecz down there."

"No, she isn't with me".

"Oh, I know she's down there".

(Pearse is angry.)

"Don't accuse me of speaking an untruth".

(Pause)

"I beg your pardon, Mr. Pearse, but, I know she is in the area".

"Well, she is not with me, sir".

"Am I to understand that your surrender will include all insurgent forces?"

"That is correct".

"Then I suggest we detain this young lady long enough for her to take your surrender order around to the other rebel commandants".

I turned to Elizabeth, "Will you agree to this?" "Yes," she said, "if you wish it". I told her I did wish it and shook her hand for the last time. "Thank you, Elizabeth".

Two officers took me by the arm, placed me in a waiting car and sped away to British headquarters where I wrote the surrender order:

(Pearse picks up a document and reads.)

In order to prevent the further slaughter of Dublin citizens, and in the hope of saving the lives of our followers now surrounded and hopelessly outnumbered, the members of the Provisional Government present at Headquarters have agreed to an unconditional surrender, and the Commandants of the various districts in the City and Country will order their commands to lay down arms.

Within the hour, Elizabeth O'Farrell was preparing to carry the order to the other garrisons around the city.

(Slide SR - Prisoners marching under guard.)

By Saturday night over four hundred men were under arrest. They were kept all night, with no toilet facilities, huddled on an open lawn at the top of O'Connell Street. At 9 AM on Sunday, they were marched to Richmond Barracks. On the way, they were pelted with rotten fruit and vegetables ... and chamber pots were emptied on them by the grateful people of Dublin.

I was transferred to Arbour Hill Detention Barracks where I was left in solitary confinement.

(Pearse removes his belt and lights a

candle.)

They left me my uniform but took away my belt. Perhaps they thought I might injure myself with it. More likely I would eat it for want of a good meal. But they did give me a candle and pen and paper, so I passed the hours with poems and letters, one to my brother Willie who had been with me through everything.

(Pearse sits, writes and reads.)

Of all the men that I have known on earth,
You only have been my familiar friend,
Nor needed I another.

Willie was my brother and I loved him.

I also knew my mother would be sick with worry and I desperately wanted to see her. I wrote and asked her to go to British headquarters to ask if she might be allowed to visit me. This would be my last chance to see her, my last chance to have a mother's arms hold me.

(Soundtrack: three bangs of a gavel.)

(Slides: SR - Tuesday,   SL - May 2,
Pearse stands.)

On Tuesday morning, I was taken to Richmond Barracks for my court martial. Since no defense was provided, I was allowed to address the court:

(Pearse moves centre stage.)

Now that you have heard my version of the Rising, I wish it to be understood that any admissions I make here are to be taken as involving myself alone. They do not involve and must not be used against anyone who acted with me, not even those who may have set their names to documents with me.

I admit that I was Commandant General Commanding in Chief the forces of the Irish Republic which have been acting against you for the past week, and that I was President of their Provisional Government. I stand over all my acts and words done or spoken in those capacities.

When I was a child of ten I went down on my bare knees by my bedside one night and promised God that I should devote my life to an effort to free my country. I have kept that promise. As a boy and as a man I have worked for Irish freedom, first among all earthly things. I have helped to organise, to arm, to train, and to discipline my fellow countrymen to the sole end that, when the time came, they might fight for Irish freedom. The time, as it seemed to me, did come, and we went into the fight. I am glad we did. We seem to have lost. We have not lost. To refuse to fight would have been to lose; to fight is to win. We have kept faith with the past, and handed on a tradition to the future.

I assume that I am speaking to Englishmen, who value their freedom and who profess to be fighting for the freedom of Belgium and Serbia. Believe that we, too, love freedom and desire it. To us it is more desirable than anything in the world. If you strike us down now, we shall rise again and renew the fight. You cannot conquer Ireland. You cannot extinguish the Irish passion for freedom. If our deed has not been sufficient to win freedom, then our children will win it by a better deed.

(Lights dim. Pearse returns to the table and writes.)

VOICE-OVER (President/judge)
"As President of the Courts-Martial, I have just done one of the hardest tasks I have ever had to do. I have had to condemn to death one of the finest characters I have ever come across. There must be something very wrong in the state of things that makes a man like that a Rebel. I don't wonder that his pupils adored him".

(Soundtrack: A gavel strikes three times.)

(Slides SR - Wednesday,   Slide SL - May 3.)

I was transferred to a death cell in Kilmainham Gaol where I was able to finish one final letter to my mother. With the time of execution near, a kind and gentle priest, Father Aloysius, came to administer to my needs. Before leaving, he agreed to keep a poem for my mother and, in turn, gave me this beautiful cross.

(Slides SR - Cross 1   Slide SL - Cross 2.)

On one side, with my pen, I scratched my initial, a letter "P". I knew they would be coming for me soon, so I knelt for my last prayer:

Dear God, I do not hope or even desire to live, but I do hope and desire that the lives of all our followers will be spared.
Lord, it is a grand madness when poets and schoolteachers lead the revolution. Amen.

(Pearse kisses the cross and puts it on the table.)

I would never see this cross again. At three-thirty in the morning, they came for me.

(He blows out the candle and lights dim. Soundtrack: Door closing.)

I was led through the low doorway of my cell and down the damp, dark corridors. Each metal step down to ground level echoed like a pistol shot. With no choice, I was blindfolded and my hands were bound behind my back. A soldier on each arm, I was guided out into the Stonebreaker's Yard where high walls separated the living and the dead. I could feel the rough cobble stones under my feet but I could not see the lorry near the gate which held the bodies of Clarke and MacDonagh, and I could not see their blood which stained the ground where I stood. Facing me, the twelve-man firing squad was ready, six kneeling, six aiming over their heads.

(Slides: SR and SL - Split painting of execution.)

There was no delay as the officer in charge gave the order.

VOICE-OVER

Ready!

(Sound of rifle bolts.)

PEARSE

And in that eternity that exists at the moment of death, I recalled the words I had just written:

"My Dearest Mother,

I have been hoping up to now that it would be possible to see you again, but it does not seem possible. Good-bye, dear, dear Mother. Through you I say good-bye to Margaret, Mary Brigid, Willie, and everyone at St. Enda's. I hope and I believe that Willie and the St. Enda's boys will be safe.

I have written two papers about financial affairs and one about my books, which I want you to get. With them are a few poems which I want added to the poems of mine in MS, in the large bookcase. You asked me to write a little poem which would seem to be said by you about me. I have written it, and one copy is at Arbour Hill Barracks with the other papers and Father Aloysius is taking charge of another copy of it.

I have just received Holy Communion. I am happy except for the great grief of parting from you. This is the death I should have asked for if God had given me the choice of all deaths: to die a soldier's death for Ireland and for freedom.

We have done right. People will say hard things of us now, but later on they will praise us. Do not grieve for all this, but think of it as a sacrifice which God asked of me and of you.

Good-bye again, dear, dear mother. May God bless you for your great love for me and for your great faith, and may He remember all that you have so bravely suffered. I hope soon to see Papa, and in a little while we shall all be together again.

Margaret, Willie, Mary Brigid, and Mother, good-bye. I have not words to tell my love of you and how my heart yearns to you all. I will call to you in my heart at the last moment.

Your son,
Pat.

VOICE-OVER

Aim!

PEARSE
And my mother answered. She heard me and she
answered with our poem.

> (Slide SR - Pieta 1   SL - Pieta 2
>   SR - Pieta 3   SL - Pieta 4
>   SR - Pieta 5   SL - Pieta 5 repeat)

VOICE-OVER
I do not grudge them: Lord, I do not grudge
My two strong sons that I have seen go out
To break their strength and die, they and a few,
In bloody protest for a glorious thing,
They shall be spoken of among their people,
The generations shall remember them,
And call them blessed;
But I will speak their names to my own heart
In the long nights;
The little names that were familiar once
Round my dead hearth.
Lord, thou art hard on mothers:
We suffer in their coming and their going;
And tho' I grudge them not, I weary, weary
Of the long sorrow---And yet I have my joy:
My sons were faithful, and they fought.

PEARSE
I will call to you in my heart at the last moment.

VOICE-OVER

Fire!

(As the largest Pietas fill the screens, a
volley of shots is heard. Pearse's head
drops slowly to his chest. Lights dim.
The Soldiers Song begins to play softly.)

Slide SR - Tricolor   SL -Tricolor

VOICE-OVER
We know their dream; enough
To know they dreamed and are dead;
An what if excess of love
Bewildered them till they died?
I write it out in a verse --
MacDonagh and MacBride
And Connolly and Pearse
Now and in time to be,
Wherever green is worn,
Are changed, changed utterly:
A terrible beauty is born.

(The Flag begins to blow. The anthem
builds in volume until finished. Lights
fade to black.)

THE END

An audio recording of the complete monologue, with sound effects, is now available online.

Brian Gordon Sinclair

ABOUT THE AUTHOR AND HIS WORKS

Brian Gordon Sinclair, author of *Easter Rising: The Last Words of Patrick Pearse*, is a graduate of the National Theatre School of Canada and holds a Master of Arts degree in Theatre from the University of Denver. He also studied at the Royal Academy of Dramatic Arts in London, England, and at the National Film Board of Canada.

Mr. Sinclair is the author of a seven play series entitled, *The Hemingway Monologues: An Epic Drama of Love, Genius and Eternity*. These plays detail and illuminate the life and writing of Nobel Prize winning author, Ernest Hemingway. The first five plays premiered at the Hemingway Days Festival in Key West, Florida to considerable critical acclaim. The sixth play, *Sunset* (originally titled, *In Deadly Ernest*), was commissioned by Museo Hemingway/Finca Vigia and had its world premiere at the Hemingway Colloquium in Havana, Cuba. Brian Gordon Sinclair is considered to be the foremost dramatic interpreter of Ernest Hemingway in the world today. As Patron of the children's baseball team at Museo Hemingway in Cuba, Mr. Sinclair recently co-authored *The Homerun Kid: The True Story of Ernest Hemingway's Baseball Team*.

The playwright is a proud dual citizen of Canada and Ireland. A recipient of the Sir Tyrone Guthrie Award for Acting at the Stratford Shakespeare Festival in Ontario, Mr. Sinclair has also received Awards of Distinction from Museo Hemingway and the

University of Holguin in Cuba. He has performed in Canada, Cuba, Denmark, England, Norway, Holland, Poland, Spain, the USA and at the Moscow Art Theatre in Russia.

PHOTO
GALLERY

**Pearse Pieta at Glasnevin Cemetery
Dublin, Ireland**

A visitor has left a rose on the chest of this Christ-like statue of Patrick Pearse at his gravesite.

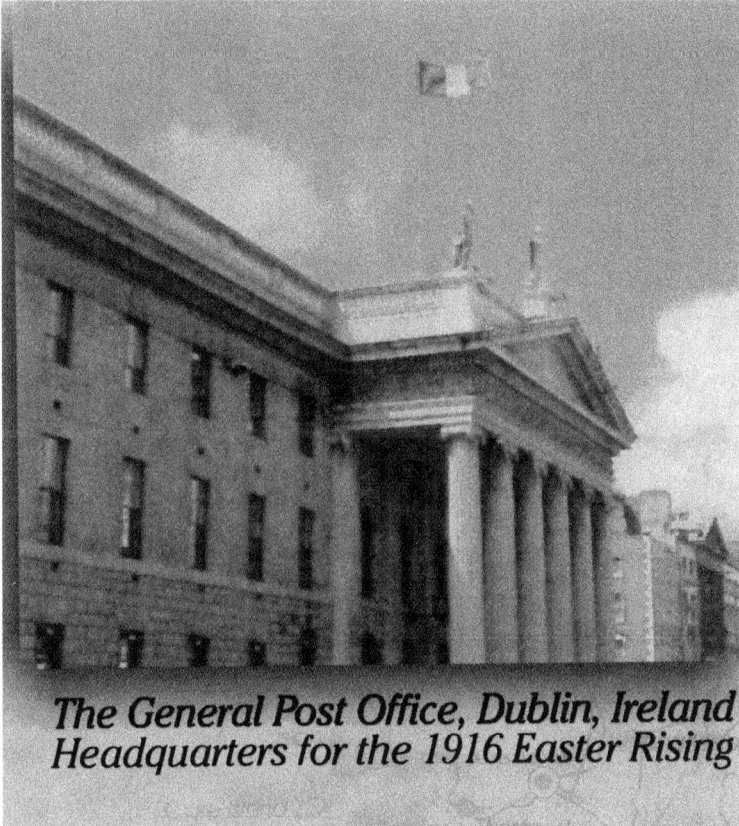

The General Post Office, Dublin, Ireland
Headquarters for the 1916 Easter Rising

If you visit the General Post Office today, you can still find bullet holes in the Greek columns at the front of the building.

The author, as Patrick Pearse, burns a dispatch.

Original brochure cover.

Full costume rehearsal.

*Original costume design created
for* Easter Rising
          by
*F. Glenn Thompson,
Artist/Historian,
Dublin, Ireland*

*Constructed by Mary Logan,
Stratford Festival, Canada*

The complete, original uniform design for Patrick Pearse, President of the Provisional Government of the Republic of Ireland and Commandant General, Commanding-in-Chief the Army of the Republic.

The sound of gunshots, both live and recorded, added
a sense of immediacy to the presentation .

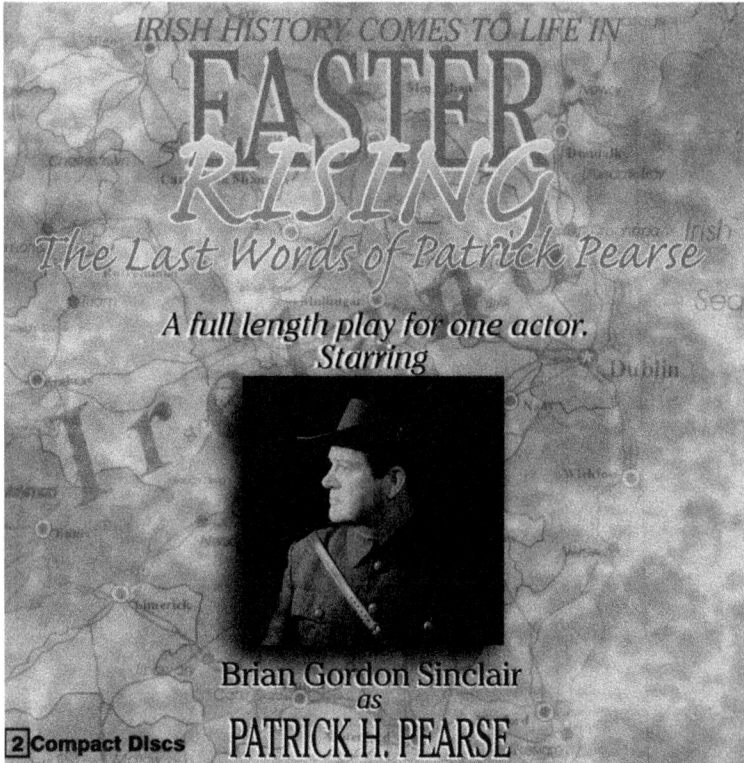

IRISH HISTORY COMES TO LIFE IN

EASTER RISING

The Last Words of Patrick Pearse

A full length play for one actor.
Starring

Brian Gordon Sinclair
as
PATRICK H. PEARSE

2 Compact Discs

The full three-act play was professionally recorded into a two CD format complete with all sound effects. The brochure design was adapted to create the CD cover.

O'Connell Street in flames.

This painting is on display inside the General Post Office in Dublin.

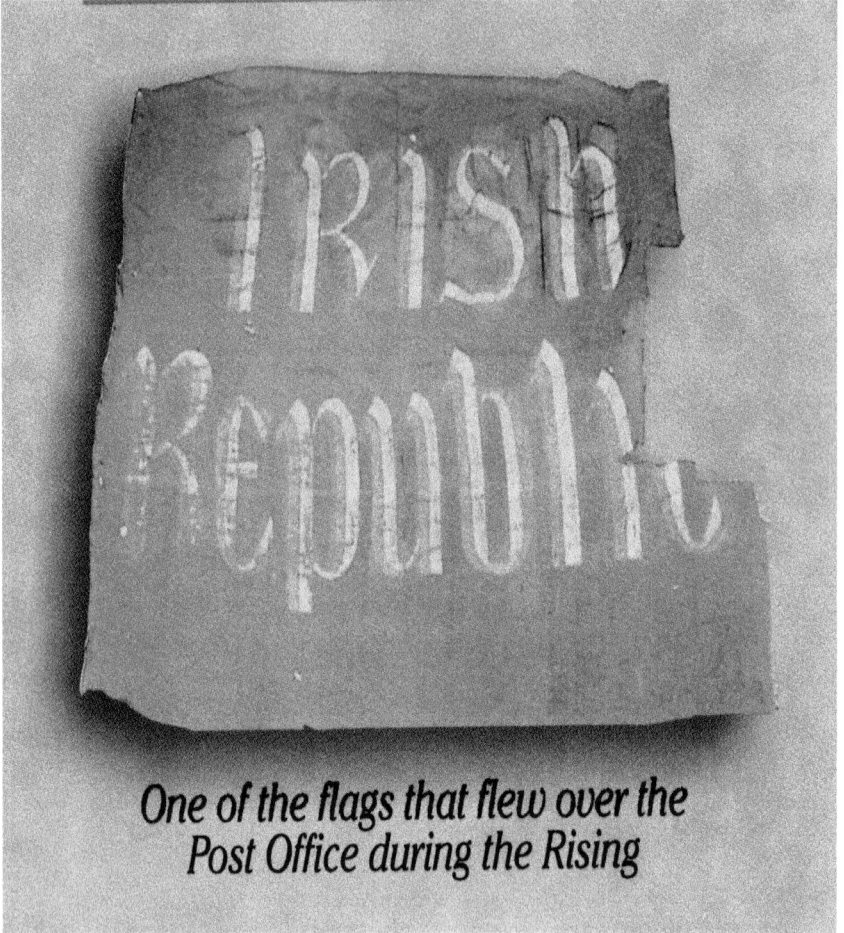

One of the flags that flew over the
Post Office during the Rising

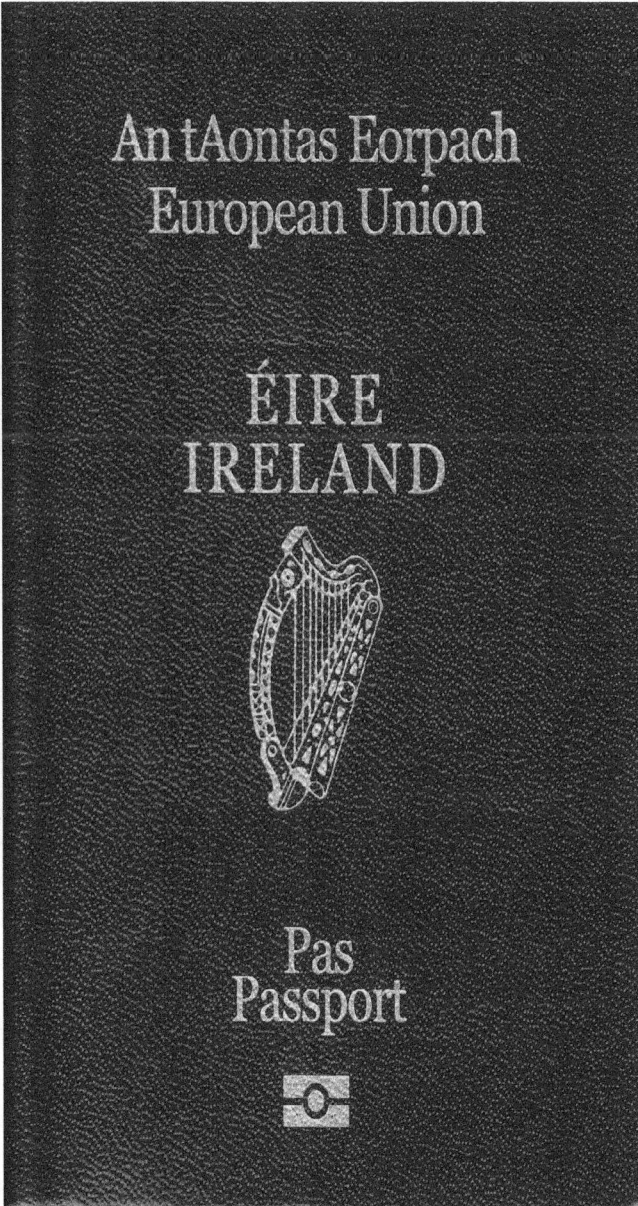

An tAontas Eorpach
European Union

ÉIRE
IRELAND

Pas
Passport

The author is a proud Irish citizen.

The author in his other persona as Ernest Hemingway. The original oil painting is by Cuban artist Elton Perez and was presented to Brian Gordon Sinclair in appreciation of his work as Patron of the Children's baseball team at Museo Hemingway/Finca Vigia.

Ernest Hemingway, like Patrick Pearse, was involved in war and revolution. Here the author is seen portraying Hemingway in the Spanish Civil War. The scene is from *The Hemingway Monologues - Part Four: The Man-Eaters*.

Brian Gordon Sinclair shares a drink with a friend, who shall remain nameless, at El Floridita in Havana, Cuba. Notice the photo on the wall. It shows a certain American author standing beside his friend, movie star Gary Cooper.

OTHER WORKS
BY
BRIAN GORDON
SINCLAIR

Sunrise, first volume of *The Hemingway Monologues,* is now available. Experience Oak Park, Illinois and Michigan as young Hemingway grows up and goes to war.

The Lost Generation, the second volume of *The Hemingway Monologues*, is also available.

"If you are lucky enough to have lived in Paris as a young man, then wherever you go for the rest of your life, it stays with you, for Paris is a moveable feast."

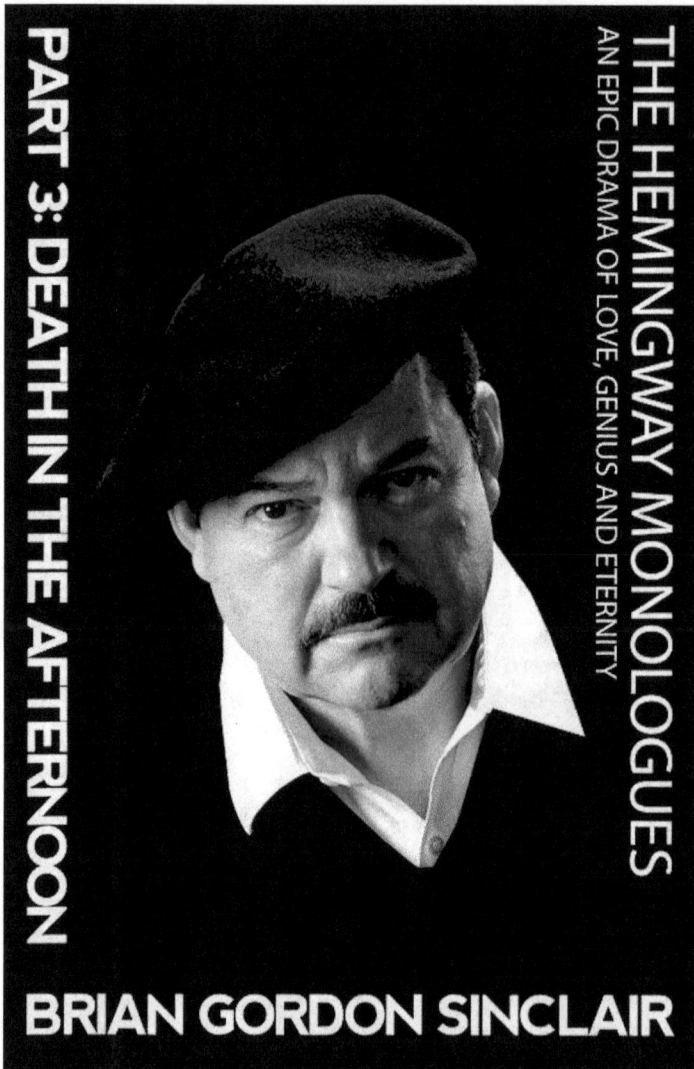

PART 3: DEATH IN THE AFTERNOON

THE HEMINGWAY MONOLOGUES

AN EPIC DRAMA OF LOVE, GENIUS AND ETERNITY

BRIAN GORDON SINCLAIR

Death in the Afternoon, the third volume of *The Hemingway Monologues*, will be available soon. Hemingway discovers the Running of the Bulls in Pamplona and confronts a devastating hurricane in Key West.

Hemingway's
HOT Havana
A Play

Brian Gordon Sinclair

Hemingway's HOT Havana is a special edition of *The Hemingway Monologues* and will soon be available in a new, revised edition. (Cover art by Robert Charles Orlin) Watch for all 7 volumes of *The Hemingway Monologues*.

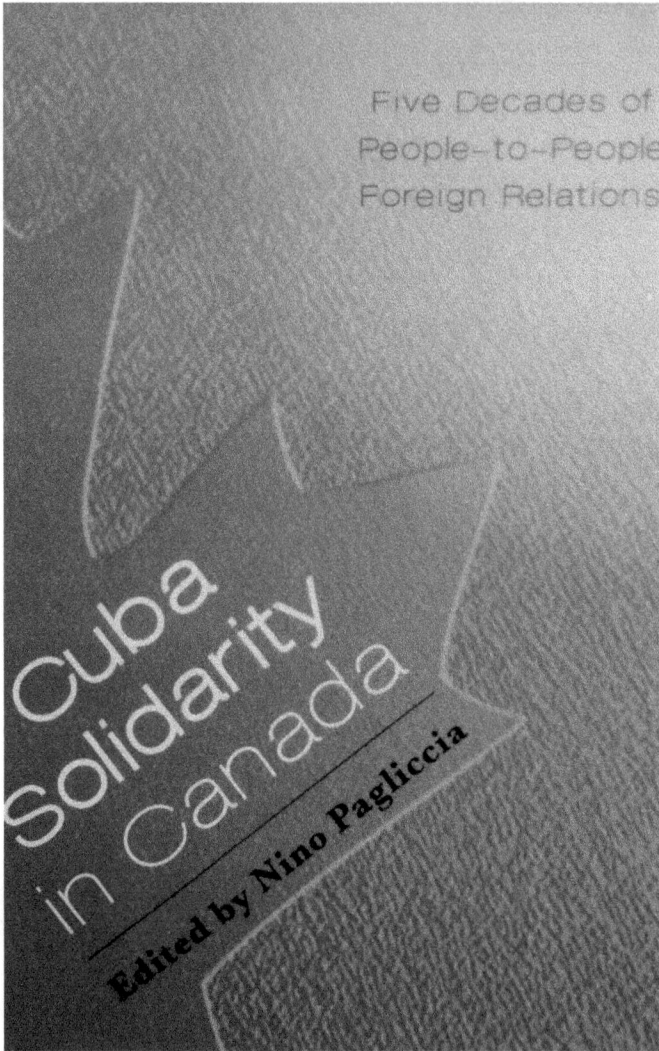

Five Decades of
People-to-People
Foreign Relations

Cuba
Solidarity
in Canada

Edited by Nino Pagliccia

I hope you will enjoy Chapter 12 entitled, "Ernest Hemingway: One Canadian's Doorway into Cuba". I speak not of politics but of love, the vibrant love of literature and people that is Cuba.

I am proud to be the official narrator and voice of *The Pirate Night Before Christmas,* Sammie Mays' fine adaption of "The Night Before Christmas". The book is available year round and my recording can be heard around the world every year during the holiday season.

THE HOMERUN KID is a brilliant memoir, told with genuine childhood innocence!

A heart-warming tribute to Ernest Hemingway. You can feel a child's love for his hero permeating every memory, every word.

THE HOMERUN KID is more than a book of children's stories. It is a valuable addition to the history of Ernest Hemingway and offers a vivid, eye-witness account to scholars and aficionados.

THE HOMERUN KID should be read to young people in every library and classroom in the world!

THE ART OF STORYTELLING AT ITS FINEST!
From the true stories of Cayuco "Jonronero" the Homerun Kid

Translation by Susana Hurlich
Adapted and edited by Brian Gordon Sinclair
$14.95

ABSOLUTELY AMAZING eBOOKS

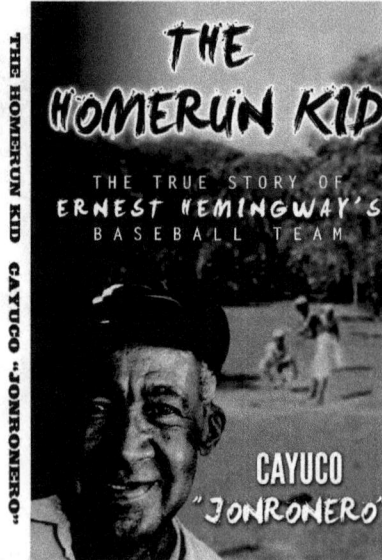

THE HOMERUN KID CAYUCO "JONRONERO"

THE HOMERUN KID
THE TRUE STORY OF
ERNEST HEMINGWAY'S
BASEBALL TEAM

CAYUCO
"JONRONERO"

In adapting the stories of Cayuco "Jonronero", I have attempted to enter into his mind and to feel as he felt. The stories, told from the viewpoint of a child through the luxury of historical perspective, appear simple but they are rich in the complexity of compassion. I knew that was true when the writing and reading of the stories brought tears in the most positive of ways. The lessons were valid in the 1940's and are no less valid today. Thank you Cayuco for allowing me to share your life. The experience has been both heart-warming and richly rewarding.

The Homerun Kid is available now.

SPECIAL INVITATION

ANNUAL EXHIBITION GAME AND HOLIDAY CELEBRATION

HISTORY OF THE ESTRELLAS DE GUIGUI/ GIGI ALL-STARS BASEBALL TEAM

In the 1940's, a children's baseball team was formed to provide an activity for Ernest Hemingway's sons when they visited their father. It was named after Ernest's youngest son Gregory, also known as Gig and Gigi. During this time, Hemingway provided uniforms, equipment and drove the kids anyplace they could arrange a game. At Christmas the children were invited to Finca Vigia (Lookout Farm), the Hemingway estate, where Ernest would tell stories to the children and give each one a present.

Approximately six years ago, the Director of Museo Hemingway (Ada Rosa Alfonso Rosales) and Oscar "Cayuco" – the Homerun Kid – Blas, the 86 year old surviving member of the original team, decided to revive the team known as the Estrellas de Guigui (the Gigi All-Stars). It has been my pleasure to assist with that revival. In December of 2013 (helped by Papa Wally Collins of the Hemingway Lookalike Society), I not only had the privilege of arranging uniforms and equipment for the team but I also revived the storytelling tradition along with the presentation of a gift to each child. Each player received a card containing one dollar and a copy of the book from which the story was taken. Naturally, the book and story vary from year to year. So far, the children have received copies of *The Homerun Monologues, The Pirate Night Before Christmas* and *The Homerun Kid*. Many more books are to come.

As Patron of the Gigi All-Stars, I invite you to join us for the Annual Exhibition Game and Holiday Celebration. The event is held yearly at Museo Hemingway in San Francisco de Paula on the outskirts of Havana and takes place on the first Saturday of every December. Admission to the event is complimentary and includes a tour of the ten-acre Hemingway estate. Hemingway, baseball, literature children and Christmas – the perfect combination. See you there next December.

Brian Gordon Sinclair
Patron

Question?

Contact Hemingway On Stage

sinclair4814@rogers.com
www.briangordonsinclair.com

P.O. Box 337
Alliston, ON, Canada
L9R 1V6

REVIEWS

"Brian, with his rich, mellow voice is a superb storyteller! He treats listeners to a wonderful stirring evening of theatre. Never has history seemed so enthralling and exciting."

     - Martin Donlevy, Toronto Irish News"

"It is a riveting performance."

     - Susan Stein, The Scope

"Sinclair has written, directed and performed this superb re-enactment of the tragic and short-lived rebellion."

"All come to life in Sinclair's splendid reading as Patrick Pearse."

A "passionate, dramatic rendering of the Easter Rising"...

     - Sharon Greer

"His [Sinclair's] own voice is exciting, his delivery dramatic and measured. His is an exciting, moving interpretation of Irish history, not without humour and, above all, immensely human."

     - AudioFile Magazine

"This production, written, directed and performed by Brian is like nothing you have ever seen about the 1916 Rising ... the most lasting impression is the on-stage presence of Sinclair himself. As he tells

107

the story of the Uprising, you are transported back in time to those few heroic days that would eventually bring about the establishment of the modern state of Ireland. It is no small measure the talent of the actor that allows you, for a short period of time, to forget that he is indeed a mere thespian and not the great man himself."

    - Viv D'Arcy, Canadian Irish Press Magazine

"It is, however, Sinclair's dramatic delivery that has incredible impact. He becomes the character exuding passion as he summons Irish men and women to their flag to strike for freedom."

"Sinclair manages to present this incredible and tragic story without depressing the audience. There is something uplifting about the hope and sacrifice of Pearse."

    - Kathryn Mooij, The Herald

EASTER RISING
NOW AVAILABLE AS AN AUDIO BOOK

EASTER RISING:
THE LAST WORDS OF PATRICK PEARSE

is now available in AUDIO BOOK format for a new listening adventure. This downloadable recording contains all three acts of the premiere stage production while maintaining the artistic integrity and emotional power of the original.

EASTER RISING presents a day-by-day account of one of Ireland's greatest historical events as told, for the first time, by Patrick Pearse himself. The recording of this seminal event is suitable for both home and educational environments. EASTER RISING ranks among the great dramas of the Twentieth Century and we are pleased to make it available to every student of Irish history and every lover of theatre throughout the world.

Quilted Celtic Cross
Designed and executed by Shirley D. Spencer
for the original production of
Easter Rising: The Last Words of Patrick Pearse.

The New Atlantian Library